# The Call of Isis

## Books by
## The Rev. Lawrence Durdin-Robertson

The Religion of the Goddess

God The Mother

Life in the Next World

The Goddesses of Chaldea, Syria, and Egypt

Women in the Arts, Crafts and Professions

Idols, Images and Symbols of the Goddesses, Egypt pts 1,2,3

Idols, Images and Symbols of the Goddesses of India

Idols, Images and Symbols of the Goddesses,

South East Asia and Tibet

Idols, Images and Symbols of the Goddesses, China and Japan

The Symbolism of Temple Architecture

The above are all by Cesara Publications

The Year of the Goddess, A Perpetual Calender of the

Fellowship of Isis (Aquarian Press)

Readers may also find the following books useful:

The Pillar of Isis by Vivienne O'Regan (Aquarian Press)

Elements of the Goddess by Caitlin Matthews (Element)

Essential Woman by Murry Hope (Mandala)

# The Call of Isis

by
**Olivia Robertson**

**NEPTUNE PRESS**
**49a Museum Street, London WC1A 1LY**

Front cover illustration *Isis* by Judith Page
Back cover illustration of the *Winged Isis* by
Sue Barrowclough (photo Ruth Bayer)
Additional drawings are by the author
Back cover photograph of a temple shrine with statue
of Juno is by Vivienne O'Regan


First published by Cesara Publications 1975
Huntington Castle, Clonegal,
Enniscorthy, Eire.


Printed in Great Britain by
Booksprint, Bristol

# Dedication

We Honour the Goddess of
Ten Thousand Names
She who is crowned with the Stars,
Is robed with the Sun
And standeth upon the Moon.

## Acknowledgements:

Sue Barrowclough, Ruth Bayer, Karl Duncan, Ingrid Fischer, Boyd Lees,
John Merron, Judith Page, Chesca Potter and Elizabeth Taylor.

## About the cover illustration:

The cover painting shows Isis standing on the moon, cloaked with the stars, and lit by the glow of the sun. Close attention was paid to the Papyrus of Ani, (the scribe), in the British Museum. This is the Book of the Dead of the noble priestess Anhai. The creator of this Papyrus painted the tunic of Isis in green. Egypt at that time did not possess the secret of making green dye. The gold collar, copied from the Papyrus, represents the 'Five Bodies'. On her head she wears the throne, early symbol of Isis, and she carries the lotus wand and gold ankh, symbol of life, as depicted in the Papyrus.

The stars include Sirius and the Pup, Orion, and the entire Zodiac starting with Leo through to Virgo, plus the constellation 'Ophiuchus' which crosses the Zodiac between Scorpio and Sagitarius.(The constellations are shown as blue stars.)

Isis is shown on the cover walking forward through time, into the future. She is painted in a naturalistic way, and not in the stylised Ancient Egyptian manner because although we honour the Ancient Egyptian Gods, we live in a different time, and are bringing the ancient mysteries into the present and on to the twenty-first century.

# Contents

## The Call of Isis

### Part One: The Temple of the Moon Goddess

### Part Two: The Temple of the Sun Goddess

### Part Three: The Temple of the Star Goddess

# The Manifesto of the Fellowship

Growing numbers of people are rediscovering their love for the Goddess. At first this love may seem to be no more of an inner feeling. But soon it develops: it becomes a longing to help the goddess actively in the manifestation of her divine plan. Thus, one hears such enquiries as, "How can I get initiated into the Mysteries of the Goddess? How can I experience a closer communion with her? Where are her nearest temples and devotees? How can I join the priesthood of the Goddess?" , and many other such questions.

The Fellowship of Isis has been founded to answer these needs. Membership provides means of promoting a closer communication between the Goddess and each member, both singly and as part of a larger group. There are hundreds of Iseums and thousands of members all over the world, since the Fellowship was founded in 1976 by Lawrence, Pamela, and Olivia Durdin-Robertson. Membership is free.

The Fellowship is organised on a democratic basis. All members have equal privileges within it, whether as a single member or part of an Iseum or Lyceum.

The Fellowship respects the freedom of conscience of each member. There are no vows required or commitments to secrecy. All Fellowship activities are optional: and members are free to resign or rejoin at their own choice. "The Animal Family of Isis" is listed in every Isian News.

The Fellowship reverences all manifestations of life. The

Rites exclude any form of sacrifice, whether actual or symbolic. Nature is revered and conserved.

The Fellowship accepts religious toleration, and is not exclusivist. Members are free to maintain other religious allegiances. Membership is open to all of every religion, tradition and race. Children are welcomed, subject to parental consent.

The Fellowship believes in love beauty and abundance. No encouragement is given to asceticism.

The Fellowship seeks to develop psychic gifts, happiness and compassion for all life.

The College of Isis has been revived after its suppression 1500 years ago. Like Aset Shemsu, the FOI itself, it has always been alive in the inner planes. It is from these inner planes that its return has been inspired. As the College of Isis is part of the Fellowship, the ideals of the Manifesto apply. The qualities of Goodness, Harmony, and Wisdom are manifested through a multi-religious, multi-racial and multi-cultural Fellowship which honours the good in all faiths. Magi degrees may be conferred through Lyceums of the College. There are no vows nor secrecy. Correspondent courses are offered.

Iseums are the very hearths of the Goddess to whom they are dedicated. They are listed, along with Lyceums and new members, in every issue of Isian News. Each Iseum is dedicated to a particular Goddess - or Goddess and God. The Fellowship of Isis Priesthood is derived from an hereditary line of the Robertson family from Ancient Egypt. Priestesses, priests, every member, have equal honour. Priestesses and priests work with the Goddess - or Goddess and God - of their own faith. Every Human, animal, bird and tree is an eternal offspring of the Mother Goddess's Divine Family of Life.

# INTRODUCTION

AT the end of an Aeon and the beginning of the Space Age the Goddess Isis is manifesting as the feminine expression of Divinity. This is necessary as patriarchal culture has dominated the world through the logical scientific mind and strong arm of man. Though this was not evil in the past, the rapid technological development has now brought the whole earth to a flash-point of catastrophe. Roughly a third of the air, seas, and land are polluted. Not deliberately, but by greed, stupidity and lack of love for nature.

The principles of patriarchal religion have set mankind against nature and created a war with the flesh. The Divine Plan of the Goddess, by whatever name you know her, is to restore harmony: the Goddess does not subtract, she adds. She is not fighting patriarchy, she is re-introducing matriarchy. This is a loving way - a love for all beings which particularly belongs to the Mother, for the universe itself gives birth to all that is and may aptly be called the Cosmic Matrix. Therefore however humble we are on our planet, we are allowed to co-operate with the Goddess in restoring the earth to that heaven that it should be in communion with the other spheres of being beyond the senses. Mankind dies but the spirits of humanity are immortal, therefore the Goddess of Love, Beauty and Truth brings happiness, harmony and psychic gifts.

The Great Goddess was adored by the Ancient Egyptians as Aset, perfect daughter of the Star Goddess Nuit and the Earth God Geb.

The Hellenic culture used the myth of Isis to form a mighty Goddess religion in which Isis had ten thousand names, as Lucius

Apuleius, Her priest, described it. She represented all Goddesses and was in perfect balance with her consort, the God Osiris. Isis kept the flame of compassion alive during the Christian era as the Virgin Mary: Isis bore Horus in a virgin birth. The titles of Isis were bestowed on Mary by the Catholic Church: Star of the Sea, Sedis Sapientis (Seat of Wisdom), Regina Coeli (Queen of Heaven). Since 1830 She has appeared in apparitions, usually to children, and always bringing a message of love, promise of heaven and a call to penitence.

When my brother Lawrence, a clergyman, and I, were called by the Goddess to found the Fellowship of Isis in 1976, we chose to dedicate it to She who had inspired our work. It is curious that my cousin Robert Graves wrote about the Goddess long before Isis called us. She is calling people all over the world through many religions and cultures. Therefore we are a multi-religious, multi-cultural, multi-racial Fellowship. All the Goddesses are represented by the magical name I.S.I.S., and Osiris represents all Gods.

We are now moving into a greater sphere of awareness of the cosmos. This change is happening all over the world as we know here at Clonegal Castle from the letters we receive.

I have just received a letter from a Nigerian Priest of the Cosmic Isis Amaseri, who speaks of the happiness, healing, hope and psychic gifts all the members of his Iseum receive from the Divine Mother. To quote Elizabeth Barrett Browning, "There is no Death, Love is Eternal".

*Olivia Robertson April 1993*

# THE ALCHEMY OF ISIS

## CAROLINE WISE

THE last twenty years have witnessed a huge revival of the religion of the Goddess, the feminine aspect of divinity that has been neglected for so long by the dominant world religions. Now She has asked to be revealed again, presumably because we have put the earth in such great peril through the abuse of nature and of our souls.

Many people today have heard the call of the Goddess. They have retrieved Her from the labyrinths of Holy Books, mythologies, archaeology, sacred song and dance, and also through direct psychic contact. This tangle of information has been unravelled by a new priesthood, drawn from the many strands of Ariadne's silken thread. The Goddess shows us a different way of looking at the world, a new direction and a new focus. By following her ways that silken thread is transmuted into pure gold. This is the Alchemy of Isis.

Isis of Ten Thousand Names is so named because She represents all Goddesses, some well known, others beginning to flower again like oases in a desert. Isis was the principal Goddess of the Egyptians, but her worship spread south and west into Africa via the Upper Kingdom, and into the Middle East via the Lower Kingdom. The coming of the Macedonian Greeks under Alexander the Great and the development of Ptolemaic Egypt as a consequence spread Her worship even further. Indeed it is from the Greeks that we gain the name Isis, their version of the Egyptian *Auset*. Isis was much worshipped in Alexandria, where Alchemy first spread to secular scholars, and She dictates Alchemical secrets in the Hermetic works attributed to Hermes Trismegistus, the foundation documents of all subsequent Alchemical exploration. The coming of the Roman Empire spread Her worship throughout Europe and both Libya and London boasted temples to Her. It is during this period that Isis became identified with all Goddesses, an identification which continues today.

The Mysteries of Isis practiced in the Graeco-Roman period centred around many themes. She symbolised resurrection, in that She raised through Her magic great Osiris, Her Husband, when He had been slain by Set. They also centred around fertility and prosperity, since Osiris was a Corn God, and his annual resurrection was the birth of the new crop from the black earth of Egypt, known in Roman times as the Bread-basket of the Empire. The sharing of sacred bread to celebrate resurrection was later adopted by Christianity. Isis became associated with truth, nature, love and beauty as She absorbed the aspects of other Goddesses, becoming the most universal Goddess of all. She presides over land and sea, becoming patroness of navigation, whom sailors knew as the Isis of Ships. The female figureheads on the prows of ships have their origins in Isis: She was Stella Maris, Star of the Sea, a title later transferred to the Virgin Mary.

In Her winged form She became associated with the realms of the air and the notion of flight, and this association with all forms of transport, both ancient and modern, is very much alive in the Fellowship of Isis today as it reaches out from Ireland to all of the continents of the world.

The ancient name of Isis means 'throne', for she represented the rulership of Egypt, and later by extension the guardianship of all of the world, throughout the cycle of the year. These transformations in Her role are as much a part of the Alchemy of Isis as those changes that She brings to those She touches.

Many of these concern matters beyond the physical. She controls the activation of the Kundalini, or 'serpent power' in the opening of the psychic centres. She also taught the other deities knowledge of the stars, and many of those who have experienced psychic transformation through visions of Her speak of Her coming from the stars. It is no co-incidence that so many UFO contactees speak of a woman of divine grace imparting wisdom to them, for this was always her role, whatever form the vehicle was seen to take, and whatever the literal truth of these encounters. Isis is, after all, daughter of the Star Goddess Nuit.

Those who work with the Goddess in Her myriad forms will discover that the only thing that is constant is constant change! Isis is Mistress of Magic, said to be greater than a thousand magicians. As Mistress of Egypt, the land first known as Khem, She has now brought her Alchemy (named for Her land) to the thousands of members of the Fellowship of Isis. They have experienced major life changes, an explosion of creativity, a change in the direction of their life, increased psychic abilities and deeper insights into the mysteries and also into their everyday life.

The Fellowship of Isis is now a major force in the international movement for the renewal of the religion of the Goddess. To understand how this came to be we must look into the way that She revealed Herself to the founders of the Fellowship.

The Temple of Isis at Clonegal Castle is the Foundation Centre of the Fellowship. This castle is the ancestral home of Lawrence Durdin-Robertson and Olivia Robertson, his sister. It lies in a valley encircled by hills and a beautiful violet mountain. It is magically positioned between two rivers, at their confluence. The Derry, named after the Oak tree, and the Slaney rush together at the place known as the Crow's Foot. This is the foot of the Macha, the Irish Mother Goddess in one of Her many guises, and there is a tradition that this was an ancient matriarchal centre for the mysteries. The joining of two rivers, whether they be the Tigris and Euphrates at the cradle of Middle Eastern civilisation; the Beckhampton and Winterbourne which are part of Avebury's landscape of the goddess; or the Derry and the Slaney, form another Alchemical symbol of the Divine Feminine, as different forces merge into a new and greater whole. They create the horns of the head-dress of Isis in Her Mother-aspect, when She is suckling the Divine Child Horus, and the cow's horns of Hathor, goddess of beauty, love and dance. They form the antlers of Elen, the Green Isis and Goddess of the trackways. The horns of the moon which hold the sun disc on the head-dress of Isis represent the feminine alchemy, as they wax and wane monthly; and antlers grow, mature and are then shed annually with the change of the season on the migratory route of the reindeer, which formed the first paths.

The path to the Temple of Isis is formed by a long avenue of Lime trees which visitors find acts as a true rainbow bridge between the mundane world and the enchanting temple, where so many experience other realms and communion with the Goddess. To one side of the avenue, in a field lent by Lawrence Durdin-Robertson to the local Gaelic Athletic Association, lies the Bullawn Stone, an ancient round megalith representing the feminine principle. A carved hollow collects rainwater which still transforms sickness into health, the local people using the water to cure their ailments. Just beyond this point in the avenue is the spot where a meteorite fell at the end of the 19th century. This celestial object, choosing to earth itself at Clonegal, glowed for four years providing a warm perch for the local crows, the birds of the Morrigan, a major Irish Goddess.

It was along this avenue that Olivia and Lawrence came as young children when they moved to Eire from Surrey in South East England. It was a physical journey that was to lead to journeys of another kind, to other worlds. Olivia remembers that at the age of eleven she was regularly helping the recently departed on their transition to the next world, the greatest transformation of all. She recalls: "I remember helping a Bishop to cross a river to the next side. His soul was like a lot of dried leaves."

In the ancient Egyptian mysteries the guide on this most dramatic of transformations, from matter to spirit, was the Goddess Nepthys, sister of Isis, the guardian of the recently departed souls. This is a task performed by many dedicated modern-day spiritualists, but Olivia at eleven had no knowledge of these things. She remembers that it wasn't the 'done thing' to talk about such matters: "Millions of people have had experience of psychic phenomena, UFOs, spirits, angels and deity. They astrally project and have visions, but they don't talk about it. It isn't because they are afraid of ridicule, but it doesn't enter into everyday existence. There is a sort of barrier between the material world now, and spirituality. In the Middle Ages one could talk about it. They either got burnt or became a saint, so it was a bit risky being a psychic in those days. But I do think people had more faith in the reality of these experiences."

Olivia found herself leading a kind of double life. In her everyday outer life she was consciously a disbeliever in psychic matters, yet at the same time she found herself helping the dead, astrally projecting, and visiting what she and Lawrence called 'extensions'. These were realms that seemed to be connected to certain physical parts of the castle. Her powers of premonition increased, and she did talk to her father, who was fairly psychic, about some of these. To herself and the outside world, however, Olivia was the sensible, down to earth girl who did brilliantly at school, liked classical music, got a scholarship to Art School and became an internationally acclaimed novelist. But she quietly continued to search for others who could commune with deity. At first she turned to Orthodoxy. She recalls: "I felt that the Anglican priesthood was now totally unable to channel spiritual power. The Roman Catholics used to be able to do it, but were now a bit ashamed, it had become vaguely 'non-U' to be miraculous. You were just meant to be a socialist and be very good to everybody. This is true, it is what Christ taught them to do, but few of them were very good at it. The Methodists were wonderful with their singing and healing, and the Hindus were past masters at it all but rather despised the psychic realm. They were into higher spirituality but I thought that the higher spirituality wasn't doing them much good as regards social reform. They have the caste system, which I found to be very deep when I got to know them better. They have the poor old untouchables, whom nobody seemed to care about except Ghandi, whom I admired immensely. The Sufis are wonderful, but they don't seem to be very tolerant of idolaters like the Hindus.

"I was interested in the Quakers for a long time. They were very good with social work and the material plane, but then they said 'the Holy Spirit has left, we don't get the Holy Spirit any more' so I suppose my attitude was that I'd go with the establishment, the Church of England, although they didn't seem to have much spiritual power, because they were good and respectable. One settled for Jane Austen and respectability. So I did try with orthodoxy."

Olivia's visitations and visions of other-worldly beings led her to ask those she assumed would be authorities on the subject to tell her more. She says: "I had a vision of an angel once, and I remember asking a Bishop about it in the House of Lords in 1952. I asked him about angels, expecting a man in his position to have some knowledge. He told me very reassuringly that I didn't have to believe in angels. What I wanted to tell him was that I knew there were angels, I'd seen one, and I wanted to have a nice chat about them! Then he said he didn't believe in miracles, but I knew there were miracles, not very often, but they did happen. He was meant to be giving people the Holy Spirit and communion, and here he was saying that he didn't believe in miracles! It struck me as a most extraordinary conversation. I was told before my Confirmation that when the Bishop laid his hands on my head not to expect anything, as nothing would happen, and of course it didn't. I don't think that the Bishop was any more capable of channelling the Melusina - the Holy Spirit - than a cup of tea. In fact a cup of tea would do it better - it would cheer you up!"

Olivia's psychic powers continued to increase, to the extent that she had to accept their reality and look elsewhere for guidance. "I was trying to find a group of people I could really join. I met the Theosophists and many groups studying the occult arts and could compare notes with them." Her spiritual path was still very male-dominated. She agreed with Ghandi and Albert Schweitzer and she believed in Christ, as she still does, as a manifestation of God: "We all are, but he did it very well", but she didn't recognise the Goddess at all at that time. She describes the effect of the initial transformation; "The Goddess comes as an absolute shock. I was always taught it was rather common to go around seeing the Virgin Mary, especially by well educated Catholics. Their attitude was that they were a bit ashamed of it. So when I began seeing apparitions it was a bit embarrassing. I remember a clergyman, in a Church of Ireland sermon, talking about the Madonna of Fatima, saying; 'And they claim to have seen the Virgin Mary, up in a tree, a very improper position for any young person to be found in.' The Protestants had this extraordinary dislike for Mary, and were dubious about the Virgin Birth, as miracles were going out of fashion, but a miracle is simply the sudden manifestation of a greater sphere into a smaller one."

Olivia's vision of the Goddess certainly began to have an Alchemical effect upon her life. She realised it was a Sangreal, a Holy Grail, symbol of the divine feminine principle.

"It came in the form of the sign of Mars, and the evil super-child, legs straddling the world, the sort of child who bullied everyone in the sand pit. Then I saw this symbol reversed and becoming the holy Grail. It was the sign of Venus, or the Ankh, the host was there, the circle of Mars but reversed over the equal armed cross, and the outline of a cup. Across the ankh or the sign of Venus were two horns, and the host, the sacred bread, was resting upon these things. Only later I recognised that these were the horns of Hathor which I used for the emblem of the Fellowship Of Isis. So the discovery of the Goddess was a bit like Cinderella's fairy-godmother revealing herself, or Venus appearing suddenly in a rock in Tannhauser."

It was to her brother Lawrence (Derry), that the truth of the reality of the Goddess first manifested. Both had read the Acts of the Apostles in their early 20s. Derry became a clergyman, and he came through his studies, and through intuition, to see 'God the Mother', the Divine Feminine. He became completely converted. Olivia comments "I was always trying to bring in the God, although my brother was *totally* for the Goddess, as was my nephew. Then I realised that it had to be like this to be totally effective. Derry didn't like the sacrifice of Christ, bloody, violent, tortured on a cross, an horrific unnatural image. But a woman gave blood monthly, naturally, as a source of life, fertility. The Mother was all-important. Derry saw that our neglect of this had brought so much horror into the world, from the Synod of Whitby, where the new Christians decreed that women had no souls, to the witch burnings where millions cruelly lost their lives. One day I found Derry unnailing Jesus from a crucifix in our chapel. I saw that the Goddess was right and his kindness told me that I should work with him on reintroducing the religion of the Goddess. It was the same kindness shown by the woman washing the feet of Christ and the mercy of the Magdalene."

This discovery of the Goddess overturned the whole of Olivia's life. The Goddess was everything she had been taught to despise as an Anglo-Irish Protestant, socialist and materialist. The shock of finding that these things were actual, that "we should take heed of the Lady up in the tree" was enormous.

Olivia was, at that time, a highly successful novelist. She had left Ireland during WWII to act as a VAD for the Red Cross. While staying with a clergyman relative in Somerset, she had seen the bombers flying to and from Coventry. Until then she had been a committed pacifist. Her old socialism and idealism were still there, but tempered by the Morrigan, the Goddess who helps men pass over after death on the battlefields. Olivia was proud to have been present in 'England's Finest Hour'.

After the war Olivia returned to Ireland and researched the street games of the Dublin slum children. She was surprised to encounter the ancient mysteries in their play. She wrote for the Irish Times, Tribune and for Radio of how ancient mystery-games had been transformed by the children's experience of poverty; the ancient game of hop-scotch, where the final goal had once been 'heaven', now finished at the GPO, since that was where their fathers went to draw the dole! She found that these games had come down via ancient traditions based on pagan ritual, from initiations into mystery cults and warrior societies; the 'piggy in the middle' that children pushed around had once been the symbol for the soul.

Olivia also investigated and wrote on the pioneers of baby therapy, including the Sister Mary Kenny technique for helping malformed children, and the work of Estrid Dane, of the British War Relief Society of the USA. Estrid Dane developed the work of the Neumann-Neurode method of exercises for infants, making the spine move freely through natural movement rather than ballet or 'physical jerks' exercises. This system had similarities with both Yoga and Eurhythmics, and the free-expression in the dance of Isadora Duncan. This led Olivia to the realization that it was good for both physical and mental health for people to project themselves. They could get rid of inhibitions which clog up the system and cause all sorts of problems, through chanting, song, and natural dance, the domain of the goddess Hathor. By free expression, children could develop their personalities and adults transform their lives.

When she turned to writing novels, Olivia was immediately successful. Her second novel 'The Field of the Stranger' was a Book Society choice and received extremely good reviews in the London Times Literary Supplement and the Chicago National Herald to name but two. This novel was set in the Irish countryside she knew so well and until the Goddess arrived Olivia played the part expected of her. She wore the usual dark browns, wore no make-up and kept her hair short, since at that time and in her circles it was not the done thing to look feminine, since femininity was equated with foolishness. Suddenly she decided to allow the inner transformation to show to the outside world. She grew her hair, astonished that she could grow so much of it, began to wear bright colours and make-up. She began to write rituals and use romantic language rather than the "very good Anglo-Saxon 'Low Dutch' English". She recalls: "I suppose I appalled my previous readership. I was told that 'Field of the Stranger' was in every country house in England. I produced my last work for orthodoxy in 1956, 'The Dublin Phoenix' for Jonathan Cape. It sold out on the first day of publication, but my star was transforming, I was changing. I felt like I was growing wings, emerging from a chrysalis. I was doing Yoga and I seemed almost to become younger. I was very short-sighted but I stopped wearing glasses and my sight improved, curiously. I started wearing black velvet and silver amulets. I suppose my friends and I, with our pre-Raphaelite look, were pioneer hippies!"

Although her experiences in the war had transformed Olivia's view on pacifism, she nevertheless feels that the Goddess began increasing the strength of her call after the explosion of the atomic bomb.

"We are gardeners of the earth, as in Eden. We are guardians looking after all the species, and are part of the great symbiosis of animal and angel. We have failed, so we are getting help from non-human realms. I am totally against duality, everything being seen as good against bad, black and white. The most horrible demons come from inside you, and so you have to transform them."

The reintroduction of the religion of the Goddess through the Fellowship of Isis has worked, and her alchemy is shaping and changing the lives of those who have answered the call. Isis in her 10000 names is being animated across the planet. Some, for instance, are following the path of Sekmet, the Lion-headed goddess who transforms war to joyous celebration; some honour Brigid, the Celtic goddess of smith-craft and poetry, who transforms mere words and base metals; others have chosen Artemis, mistress of the beasts, and strive to make the world a better place for animals, and there is a growing band working with the goddesses Gaia and Elen, dedicated to the conservation of our precious earth. Kwan Yin and Amaterasu are being heard again in the Far East. The celebration of Ngame of Africa and Lakshmi of India continues after thousands of years. Through the Fellowship of Isis, one may experience communion with, and receive wisdom from, all of these and more. The Alchemy of Isis, the ultimate transformation, is slowly but steadily changing the world.

## The Inner Spheres of the Earth, bisected by Planetry Rays. 33 centres are marked. The Matrix is the Inner Sun.

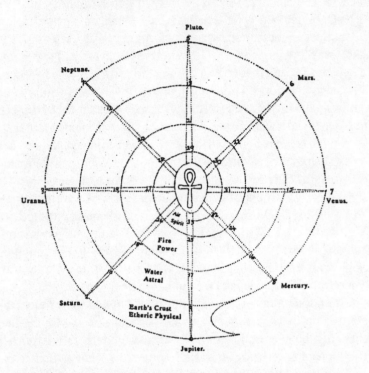

The Star and Dragon Diagram of the College of Isis depicts the four-coiled dragon, Tiamat, Goddess of Babylon, bisected by the eight-pointed star of Ishtar, the Goddess who descended and ascended all spheres to rescue Her consort Tammuz, Shepherd of the Starry Flocks. This diagram may be used to depict the coiled fire of the Life Force impregnated by the cosmic rays of divine attributes. Where the rays intersect the four planes are the points which give the 32 working, and the mystical 33rd Magi degrees of the College. We use this diagram to illustrate the development of consciousness through the spiral of Space bisected by Time.

# THE FELLOWSHIP OF ISIS

## STEVE WILSON

WHEN 'The Call Of Isis' first appeared in 1975 its readers could hardly have suspected what was to follow, but then neither the author, nor her brother Lawrence and his wife Pamela, were the type of people who let their beliefs remain as simple theory. Their family, the St. Legers, has had a long history of involvement with mysterious matters and can claim descent from Scota, legendary Queen of the Scots. They were involved with Irish Freemasonry from its beginnings in the 18th century. There is also a tradition that Cesara, a niece of Noah, came to Ireland after building her own Ark, and that her 50 maidens became the queens of the nations of the Earth. In the early 17th Century Lord Esmonde married Ellice O'Flaherty, grand-daughter of Grace O'Malley (Grainne Mhaoil) the hereditary Queen of Connaught. It seems that this ancient matriarchal line has blossomed in the Fellowship of Isis.

One ancestor, known as 'Wicked Lord Rosse' was the founder of Dublin's Hellfire Club. Legend has it that the peasants would hide, trembling, in their cottages when he and his fellow members rode to the interestingly-named Mount Venus to carry out their rites. It is said that they once roasted his butler, but this seems rather unlikely. Good servants are always difficult to find. There was another, more respectable Lord Rosse who discovered the Andromeda Nebula, now known to be a galaxy.

The family were great friends of W.B.Yeats, the Nobel Laureate, poet, and playwright, whose Celtic Twilight revived interest in Ireland's spiritual heritage and faery lore. A.E., the great Irish mystic, was another family friend. Robert Graves, whose book 'The White Goddess' has been highly influential in the revival of the religion of the Goddess, was a relative.

Lawrence had been a Vicar in the Church of England and during the 1950s had run two Churches, both dedicated to St. Mary Magdalene, in the East of England. However, he became increasingly aware of a lack of recognition for the feminine side of spirituality. His growing intuition became confirmed upon discovering the Goddess within the original Hebrew of the Old Testament. He had learnt the language in the hope of gaining a deeper understanding of the Old Testament and thus answering some of his doubts about the Church. When he realised that the first line in the entire Bible should actually read "In the beginning the Goddesses created the Heaven and the Earth" his questions were answered and he decided to follow the path of the Goddess. In 'The Call Of Isis', published before the public launch of the Fellowship, he is referred to as 'Alexander'.

His wife Pamela was a mystic with enormous feeling for nature and animal spirits. She was to insist upon the equality of all beings within the understanding of the Fellowship. Some of her mystical experience with plant spirits is recounted in 'The Call Of Isis', where she is referred to as 'Valentine.' Olivia's mystical awakening is told elsewhere in this book, but perhaps surprisingly, at first she was unsure that the Fellowship should bear the name of Isis, feeling that the masculine spirit should have its place, but Lawrence and Pamela insisted that the God had things far too much his own way already, and that a Goddess movement was needed to counter that influence.

In 1960 they had begun the Clonegal Local Welfare Society for the relief of the local poor. Lawrence regularly prevailed upon those locals who were better off to contribute, and his work was a lifeline to many in the area who were living below subsistence level. In 1963, with the introduction of a proper welfare state in Eire, this work became redundant, and the three decided to turn their attentions to relief of the spirit. As a result the Clonegal Centre for Meditation and Study was opened. This flourished throughout the 60s and 70s, and many famous speakers gave seminars there. These included Gerald Gough, Dion Fortune's successor in the Inner Light, Ross Nichols, founder of the Order of Bards, Ovates and Druids and Lady Mayo, who taught Positive Thinking and Spirituality.

From 1963 to 1974 Olivia trained as a medium and healer in London. This gave her a key understanding; that direct communication with the Goddess is vital, rather than doctrines or creeds. Above all she became convinced of the objective reality of the Goddesses and Gods, the psychic realms and supernatural, extraterrestial intelligence, at a time when many groups, perhaps in an attempt to be respectable, opted for 'psychological' theories to explain such matters. This was to play an important role when, a year after the publication of 'The Call of Isis', the Fellowship was formed on the Vernal Equinox of 1976.

Central throughout the Fellowship are certain fundamental principles. First is that the religion of the Goddess has been neglected for too long, to the detriment of the whole world. While She was present in ancient Europe, and is still followed by Asian and African societies, as well as in religions carried by them to new lands, society in general is dominated by a post-Christian culture that had stamped out Goddess worship in its Puritan phase. Whereas once the Catholic Church was able to absorb Her worship into cults centred around the Madonna and certain saints, even this was under threat. Now, more than ever, the Goddess needed to be able to bring Her gentle and caring presence into an increasingly cruel world.

A second principle was that no form of hierarchy existed. Power structures were part of the religious format of the old age. Olivia, Lawrence and Pamela did not hold power over members, neither does anyone else. Children and Animal members are considered equal in all respects. The titles that were to emerge as the Fellowship expanded describe duties and responsibilities undertaken, but not rank.

A third and vital principle was that the Fellowship was not attempting to start a *new* religion. It recognised that the Goddess was already emerging in many new areas, and that many societies had not forgotten Her. As a result, the Fellowship is a multi-faith, multi-cultural organization.

A fourth principle was that the idea of sacrifice in any form, including those understood by Christianity as the sacrifice of pleasure, was against the wishes of the Goddess. It was made clear that we are to enjoy the earth and our lives as part of Her worship.

## THE DEVELOPMENT OF THE FELLOWSHIP

To the first members of the FOI the Fellowship may have been seen as a worthy idea, worth supporting simply because of these principles. The early members were mainly people who already knew the founders through the earlier meditation centre, but Olivia began to advertise in Prediction, a British magazine with a world-wide circulation and enquiries began flooding in. It was obvious that Isis was calling to thousands of people, whereas Olivia had originally expected 'a handful' of members. They were sent the FOI manifesto and, if they returned the membership form, were immediately full members.

To those who sent a small subscription the newsletter was sent. This listed new members, including their address if they agreed, services, books, magazines and societies that members were involved with. It also listed FOI centres around the world, which at that time were mainly existing Goddess-based groups whose members had joined the FOI and registered that group with the FOI as well.

Strange as it may seem nowadays, no other such listing existed, the FOI had created the world's first Goddess Networking magazine, and one immediate effect was an incredible increase in membership. The FOI became the forum in which Pagans, Christians, Hindus, Shintoists, Druids, Witches and many others could meet, at first by letter and later in person.

Early members included the late Professor Gokale of Poona, India who was one of the first academics to realise the danger to the world caused by deforestation, and his passionate writings in defence of trees inspired many people around the world. Another was Professor Ohmuma of Japan, a Warburg Professor who brought the Goddess Amaterasu and Shinto into the FOI.

One existing group in Nigeria made an immediate and massive contribution to the FOI. This is the Church of Isis, founded by Michael Okoruwa. He was already a major religious leader in Nigeria, and to this day holds healing ceremonies so well attended that it has become necessary to hold them in football stadia! His book, *The Aour*, was the best-seller in Nigeria for several months. He had realised that many Nigerians were attracted to new faiths as they moved from the country to the city, but were turning away from the Goddesses. He founded the Church of Isis to bring them into a wider Goddess-based faith after receiving a vision of an Isian priestess. Upon learning of the Fellowship he immediately enroled the entire Church, and to this day Nigeria contributes about a third of all members of the FOI.

By the early 1980s a new development had taken place. Many of the members found that they were dissatisfied with groups that they were in. Usually this was because they had joined the only group available in their locality, and many of those in more magically-oriented group felt more religiously or mystically inclined, and vice versa. Others had no group at all, but wished to take their involvement with the Goddess further. They began asking if there could be a specifically FOI Priesthood.

Pamela, Lawrence and Olivia realised that this would be a major change. It ran the danger of making the FOI a rival to groups that so far it had succeeded in bringing together. After much meditation in the Temple of Isis at the castle, described elsewhere in this book, they decided to revive the ancient Isian priesthood, but in a totally non-denominational way. Each would be free to serve the Goddess in any way they saw fit, according to the lights of their own hearts. It was stressed that the priesthood would have no extra rank in the FOI. Priestesses and Priests would also be authorized to carry out the existing ceremonies for birth, death and marriage that had been published from the Foundation Centre.

The Priesthood was an immediate success, and one unforeseen result was that many people who were already Priests, Priestesses or with similar positions in member groups began asking for Priesthood within the FOI as well. The founders had often relied upon the recommendations of such people when others asked for this role, and they had seen the effect upon often comparative newcomers, and sought it for themselves. Priesthood, in the Fellowship, is more than a role. It brings mystic communion with the Goddess, enriching the everyday life of each Priest and Priestess. This personal, rather than social aspect, continues to bring hundreds of people to serve the Goddess. In one early case, an ordination was carried out in Ireland while the new Priestess, Morgan Benedict, was in Atlanta, Georgia with eleven members of her group. A transatlantic telephone line was used to connect the two temples, and this unique ceremony was reported in the American press.

## THE LITURGY

While this huge growth was happening, Olivia had been receiving a series of rituals during her daily meditations in the Temple. These had first been published in the FOI newsletter and were then collated in booklets. As well as the rituals for birth, death and marriage already mentioned these are, to date:

DEA: Rites and mysteries of the Goddess. This contains rites for dawn and sunset, four seasonal rites and five mysteries, one for each season and one for both autumn and winter. There is also a rite for the dedication of a shrine to Isis. These are receptive, passive rites to allow the Goddess in. Members who dislike imposing ceremonies upon ancient sites often find that the Dea rites feel acceptable at such places, since they allow the energies of these old sacred spaces to work without forcing them to fit pre-conceived notions.

URANIA: Ceremonial Magic of the Goddess. Here there are rites for space, time, the sun, moon and earth and all of the planets except Pluto. These are far more active, and by invocation create communion with the Goddesses and Gods associated with each ray. Olivia emphasises that through these rituals people come to realise that the deities are not merely archetypes but real, supernatural beings.

SOPHIA: Cosmic Consciousness of the Goddess. This contains twelve rites, one for each sign of the zodiac. These are passive, and allow understanding of the wisdom of the stars.

PANTHEA: Initiations and Festivals of the Goddess. The eight seasonal festivals of the Celts become internationally based, plus rituals for the Homing of Children, the Funeral ceremony, initiation into a fellowship centre and the Porta Mystica, representing entering a new, mystical phase of life. These are suitable for public performance, and many have been shown on Television around the world.

MAYA contains five rites created for solo use. These are of great use for members who are unable to join groups.

PSYCHE: Magical journeys of the Goddess. This takes the practitioner through the Star of Ishtar and the Dragon of Tiamat. These are trance journeys in which the practitioners create a UFO-type vehicle of light for journeys through the spheres of the heavens. Hundreds of people have been led on such journeys by Olivia at conferences and conventions

Each ritual contains an opening invocation and an oracle of the Goddess concerned, and these have been collected as SYBIL.

A new series, Melusina, is currently being published, and it consists of rites for awakening the Chakras. Many members are already reporting fantastic results from those that have already been published in Isian News.

Lawrence too began to publish an enormous amount of his life's research into the Goddess. These books are extremely well researched, preferring to give original quotations rather than interpreting them. The result of the works of Lawrence and Olivia has been an enormous wealth of material that enhances the religion of the Goddess throughout the world. This alone would be a lasting gift to the world, but the Goddess, it seems, is never satisfied.

While Olivia's rituals seemed to present a complete magical liturgy, at first many established practitioners were sceptical. They seemed to disobey certain hard and fast rules that had become rigid within the mysteries. They always included Goddesses and Gods from different pantheons, which alone was anathema to many. They were extremely elaborate, using words and gestures that sound antiquated. However, in 1986 Vivienne O'Regan and myself, having tried out one or two of these rituals, found that in fact they were extremely powerful. They worked extremely well and had a profound and beneficial effect on the practitioners. We decided to set up a group dedicated to carrying them out.

## THE COLLEGE OF ISIS

The result was the initiation of another phase in the development of the FOI. Lawrence and Olivia decided to revive the terms Lyceum and Iseum. The Iseums are those centres affiliated to the FOI as before, the Lyceums carry out the liturgy. In addition, the Priests and Priestesses, given the additional role and name of Heirophant, must carry out training for members wishing to join the priesthood.

Another Lyceum was formed almost simultaneously in the USA, and soon they began all over the world. Training courses, run both by personal tuition and by mail, sprang up everywhere. One of these has already been published, Vivienne O'Regans 'Pillar of Isis' (Aquarian Press 1992). The College of Isis, the Heirophants and the Lyceums, has moved beyond the Orders and Circles of more narrowly based groups. The personal aspect of the Fellowship allows each individual their own awakening at their own pace and the Magi Degrees were instituted to recognise this growth. Each degree is given when an FOI rite produces a mystical experience. Again, there is no cachet associated with these degrees, but they allow each individual to chart their own growth.

There are 33 degrees in all. These consist of the rituals of rebirth, ordination and marriage, the five Dea mysteries and the rituals in Urania and Sophia. The 33rd degree is spontaneous and personal rather than ritual. The 33 are mapped on the diagram created by the intersection of the eight-rayed star of Ishtar with the fourfold coils of Tiamat. There is no strict order in which the experiences may unfold. People wishing to undergo this course can either join a Lyceum or undertake one of the seven correspondence courses currently being offered by various Lyceums.

## RECENT DEVELOPMENTS

By 1990 the Goddess movement in general was growing apace. In this year Olivia asked members of a London Lyceum to organise a Fellowship of Isis event. This became the first Fellowship of Isis World Convention, when for the first time members and groups came together under the FOI banner. At the end there was a massive circle dance, where the leaders of groups which themselves had world-wide memberships were literally joined together. This seemed the high point in Olivia's, Lawrence's and the late Pamela's dream of reviving the world-wide religion of the Goddess.

However, there was still more to come. It became obvious to Olivia and Lawrence that while many members were concerned about the environment, the FOI should do something more directly. Since his recognition as Baron Strathloch Lawrence had had the right to form an order of chivalry, and in 1990 the Noble Order of

Tara was formed. Tara is both the name of the hill upon which the Kings of Ireland were crowned and the name of the major Goddess of Tibet. Each priory must devote itself to a particular local ecological campaign, and already this has led to saving Mount Leinster from strip-mining. Many other campaigns are under way.

This was followed in 1992 by the formation of the Druid Clan of Dana, named after the Irish Mother-Goddess. This is dedicated to the Druidic mysteries. Olivia and Lawrence had worked with Ross Nichols, founder and chosen chief of the Order Of Bards, Ovates and Druids, who had developed much of the OBOD course while staying at Clonegal Castle in the 1960s. They had also worked with the Herenarch of the Megalithic Order, an Irish Druid group, and Philip Carr-Gomm, the present Chosen Chief of OBOD. Since many members were growing interested in Druidism as a way of celebrating nature, the Clan was founded. Already it produces its own magazine, Aisling, is active in the Council of British Druid Orders and will organise the 1993 Druid Convention in London.

The next phase? In August 1993 the FOI will be the first Goddess-based organisation represented at the World Parliament of Religions. This is to be held in Chicago on the 100th Anniversary of the first Parliament. FOI members from all over the world and from many different Goddess-based faiths will attend. The Goddess will at last take her place in the faiths of the world.

Will this be enough? I doubt it. Whatever the Goddess intends will be done, of that we can be sure. The FOI has grown from three people with a common dream to become a vehicle for the Goddess, through which she has reached into the hearts and lives of many thousands of people.

# PART ONE

# TEMPLE OF THE MOON

*'She felt herself falling into it'*

# CHAPTER 1

# THROUGH THE VEIL

CHILDREN were playing on a grassy slope. On the one side they were bounded by a privet hedge newly clipped; on the other three sides by the potting-shed wall, the yard wall, and the house. The garden had run to seed with long grass and wild flowers. One of the children had separated herself from the others, and had wandered off on her own - she did not know why. Her companions' calls grew fainter.

Suddenly her attention was attracted by a flower growing by itself. It was a flower she had not noticed before. It was brilliant scarlet, with a grey furry stalk. She knelt down and examined it more closely. It had a thick heady smell. Within it were black velvet spikes, set tidily in a circle. She held the long rough grey stalk and gazed deep into the flower. The black centre with its radiating spokes began to revolve, at first slowly, then more quickly. As it did this, the sounds of the other children playing stopped; and so did the song of the blackbird in the neighbour's apple tree. Instead she heard a low humming sound like the buzz of a bee. The flower grew bigger and bigger, and the centre grew into a black tunnel and she felt herself falling into it . . .

When they found the girl's body the children were afraid, for she lay face downwards, stiff and cold. One of the younger ones screamed, and the eldest child called for her mother. And the mother had the girl carried indoors out of the sun. She was laid on her bed upstairs in the tiny bedroom she shared with her older sister.

The father rang for the Doctor. He said she was in a coma, and had she done this before? And the mother looked embarrassed, and said that the little girl was a day-dreamer: and that her aunt was a medium and used to go into trances. Not on her side of the family, she added quickly, but it was there on the father's side.

Meanwhile the girl, as she fell down the tunnel, remembered Alice in Wonderland who had, she remembered, done much the same thing, so she did not mind. There must be an end to this falling. And so there was. She landed still in darkness, on earth, and looked about for the White Rabbit. She could not see any such person, but before her was a long dark passage with a light at the far end. She picked herself up, and wondered what size she was now, because, she thought, I must be very small if I can fall through a flower. Or perhaps I'm the same size as usual and the flower suddenly got bigger, like in science fiction stories.

When she reached the end of the tunnel, she came out into a beautiful garden, full of trees and flowers. What was strange about it was that all the flowers and trees seemed more alive than at home, as if they could talk. But as this girl had followed Alice's adventures through the Looking Glass she accepted this calmly. She just thought how sensible of her parents to give her a book so helpful in such circumstances.

Then she saw the boy. He was standing, legs apart, hand in pockets, gazing at her.

"Hello!" he said. "Have you just come?"

"Yes" she said.

"How?"

"Oh, I fell through a strange flower in our garden."

"I was just crossing the road. You can say I came by bus." And he laughed. "That was a joke".

"I can't see anything funny about that," said the girl. And because she liked to understand everything very clearly, she began to feel afraid. She wondered how she could get home to tea. As she thought that, suddenly the lady came. She felt she had seen her before. The lady said; "It is time to come home," very clearly. But the girl wanted to play with the boy. But he just waved and ran across a small stream by a wooden bridge. The girl tried to run after him, but the lady took her by the hand. Then came the curious feeling of falling into the tunnel she had experienced before. But this time she did not like it. It felt stifling. And at the end, instead of the lovely garden, she found herself in total darkness, unable to move. Her eyelids felt glued together. She tried to shout, and could not. Her arms and legs felt like wood. But she did hear a voice or rather two voices.

"She is coming round," said her mother's voice.

"She is coming back," said a lady's voice.

At last she stopped struggling, and then she could open her eyes. And it was daylight and she was in bed. Her mother sat by her, and, seated next to the looking-glass, was her aunt. The girl felt she had seen her recently, but could not remember where. But she did remember the garden and the boy. And she wept bitterly. For she had heard the call of Isis, the Veiled One. Never again would she be content with children's play.

This is the story of Persephone, and of every human soul that reaches beyond the mundane.

In childhood we may enter the psychic realm with ease. A friend of mine, Angela, told me that when she was a little girl she found a doorway between two trees. It was a steamy sunny August day. She found two trees and stood between them. She said that between the trees in front of her appeared to be a mist or veil. When she crossed between the trees, she entered into a different world. The inhabitants, she said, were either very ugly or very beautiful. They were kind to her and liked to play. Possibly, she said, they understood that she was very unhappy at home. But, after some time - and time seemed to go very quickly there - they brought her back through the trees. And after that she visited the other world, until the age of ten.

Although these experiences were clearly of a psychic nature, on one occasion there was an inexplicable juxtaposition of two spheres that upset our neat classifications. For this time, when she came back to the earth plane, she did not go through the tree doorway, but instead found herself inside the pig-sty! This was a disused pig-sty, and her father kept it padlocked from the outside. She had to wait for a long time before she was discovered - and her father could not understand how she got there. And, wisely, she did not try to explain.

Some places have a strange atmosphere that seems to belong to both spheres at once. The veil between this world and the sphere of the soul seems to be thinner there. When I was eight, I was brought to such a place in Ireland. The transition from Reigate in Surrey to a South Ireland valley was in itself fantastic.

In Reigate I had lived my mundane and orderly life along with my sister and two brothers. I was receiving an intellectual education, and had faith in commonsense. Naturally I did not believe in fairies. Scientific truths used to be explained to me by my father at the breakfast table with the aid of mustard-pots and salt-cellars. I could play chess of a sort when I was five! Admittedly my sister and I were interested in the nature of time and where the past disappeared to - and how to capture 'now', but scepticism had set in very early as regards the miraculous. The atmosphere of our sensible home "Hatherlow" precluded the weird and the supernatural. Cosiness filled that existence. There was the walk to a nice school, a penny bus ride back to the Yew-Tree Inn stop. Everything was understandable. The warmth and shelter of Anglo-Saxon England was about me. It was safe.

Safe, that is, save for my sister's wild imagination. She was in love with Heathcliffe from the alien world of Wuthering Heights, and she tried to enrich her imagination-starved world with dreams. Too much so, for parents at the nice school sent a protest to the Headmistress, saying that my sister was giving the other children nightmares. Our parents were duly admonished. I do remember some of Barbara's tales. One concerned a headless nun haunting lone passages. Oddly enough, though, it was the dreadful Boiled Owl and the Guinea-pig that used regularly to send me into night-time screams. I don't know why, but even now the words have an uncanny sound. Barbara and I shared a room, and our nurse had pricked holes in the weather-streaked green blind for ventilation. These pin-pricks glittered when the light was turned off. And these, Barbara would inform me, were the horrific eyes of the Boiled Owl and the Guinea-pig watching me . . .

However, if Barbara introduced me to the macabre, I am ever grateful to her for making my first doorway into the psychic sphere. These imaginative doorways are best created by someone with a strong imagery - but more easily entered into by a passive character. And I was a day-dreamer. So Barbara told me that the green blind that I knew in daytime covered a window overlooking a road - at night was a mysterious wood. This wood, she said, was a border country through which one passed in order to reach the domain of 'Queen' Jupiter. The twinkling lights through the blind were now the lights of fairyland - if only one could get through the dark wood. How glorious and happy it was in Fairyland! It was the land of Heart's Desire - and to us infinitely preferable to living in Reigate! But always there was the wood that made a barrier both to getting there, and to getting safely back. But when we all of us arrived at the Castle in Ireland, we seemed to be half-way to the mysterious wood already. It was as if we were in the outskirts of the wood, and through the trees could see the golden and green fields and the blue hills of another sphere. The isolation of the valley added to this impression. As the Castle had been built for protection, it was situated between two rivers. It was built with six-foot thick walls over a fifteen-foot well. To us it was as if we had the Celtic 'Well at the World's End' in our very house. We were surrounded by hills, and overlooked by our blue mountain, Mount Leinster and her foot-hills.

Above all, there were the trees. The sombre yew walk girded us about on three sides, and on the other side were the ruins of 'The Abbey'.

People said ghostly monks walked up and down the yew walk, hoods up, hands clasped, using it as a cloister. For cloistered we were. And the Bullawn stone, a huge granite boulder near the lime avenue, contained a hollow that, when filled with rain-water, brought a cure for warts!

However, the house itself provided its own psychic doorways. It was only when I was grown-up that I found my elder brother also used to have a succession of dreams about 'extensions.' For instance, the old 1625 fireplace in the hall was a doorway. During the day it was just a fireplace. But not so at night. Then, heart in mouth, one found oneself in a dream going through to an extension. The extension usually was like another wing of the house, with different furnishings and inhabitants. Years later, new children in the Castle visited these extensions in dreams. Encouraged to investigate further, they would report on period, costume and architecture.

One of the most significant of these real dream experiences

came to me as a girl, when I went through the hall into an extension that was formed by a long tapestry-covered passage. I was afraid of what lurked behind the tapestries, and was careful to keep well to the middle of the passage, arms tightly to my side. But on this occasion at the end of the passage I came, not to strange rooms, but to another world altogether. It was brilliant with sunshine. I found myself watching a young man with brown rough hair busy doing magic. I knew it was magic. He was strongly muscled and naked to the waist, and was wearing what looked like a cloth tied round his waist. He was doing magic with his arms spread out, using a dance-like walk. I watched with interest.

Then I noticed a mosaic-paved fountain and people sitting round it watching me. One was an elderly man with a thin white beard and blue gown. I became aware I was trapped. However, I talked my way out of the difficulty, and the people became friendly. They played me some very curious music. Then I went back home. This experience made such an impression on me that I told my father about it at breakfast.

Nonetheless, these occasional 'magic' dreams were sporadic and beyond my control. With most children, the power to cross the threshold of the magic door disappears at about twelve years old, when the hold of earth life becomes stronger. And with many children, this should be so. The powerful evocation of the fairy-tale, the George MacDonald world of the Enchantress, give place to stories of 'real' life, of career and marriage.

Is it that the lunatic, the romantic lover and the poet alone retain their hold on the world of the unseen? Are they too old and yet too young for their fellows? For when their comrades go forth into the sunlight, they stay behind in a darkened room and look through the reflected world of the mirror into a shadow world of the imagination. For no real woman can be as perfect as the Ideal dimly seen in a glass; no actual hitch-hiking journey can equal the wonderful, sometimes terrifying adventures through dark corridors beyond the senses, as the soul makes her nocturnal flights.

When the questing traveller chooses to walk the psychic path the way is chosen that leads to the sphere of the Moon. The intention, if good, will bring forth the fantastic beauty of the sphere of the psyche. If the intention be foolish or unhealthy, such journeying may lead to madness or even death. But the lure is the same. It is the call of that which is concealed by the veil of sleep and death.

In order to enter the lunar sphere it is necessary to be passive. The troubled mind, the seething emotions, can never allow the soul to pass beyond the domain of the physical. Hence the guiding vision of these spheres is of the Master levitating over a stormy sea and, because untroubled, causes the angry waves to subside. For this realm of reflections must only be approached by the pure. Purity is a negative virtue, and as such controls a negative sphere. To say 'no' to troubled thoughts, to inhibit unruly emotions, is to discriminate, to draw a circle about oneself, and within that circle to be still. So that in order to protect one's inaction, one must actively push out the irrelevant.

And this inhibiting circle, this protective veil, is the chalice, the mirror and the pool. Otherwise the soul is lost in a tumult of psychic impressions and sensations. Therefore, in order safely to enter the world beyond the looking-glass, one needs to command the power of choice. One chooses to enter this psychic sphere only at a stipulated time, and for a certain length. One chooses to return. So indiscriminate daydreaming is ruled out. When one is functioning in every-day life, one draws one's whole consciousness upon the task in hand. So when one enters the psychic realm one also should have this concentration. The circle is created, the focussing material is at hand; crystal, glass or bowl of water. One is ready to begin one's chosen art.

*The dragon that Roderick crawled under*

# CHAPTER 2

# OF DRAGONS
# AND MARES' NESTS

A MAN is lying in a trance on the 1830 couch in the Castle library.
I am seated by him, notebook ready. I have through suggestion
conducted him into a land of vision where he has the power to
choose his own way. Now, semi-conscious, he can only hear my
voice, a voice that guides if necessary. I give advice that responds
to his words as he describes his psychic adventure. The experience,
he tells me later, has about a quarter of the reality of waking life.
But, unlike a vivid dream, he will remember it afterwards. So far in
this session all has gone well. Roderick's aim is to be a Knight of
the Grael; his chosen character, Sir Percival. His body, that of a
strong middle-aged man, is dimly seen in the golden half-light of an
autumn evening that filters through heavy Victorian curtains. But
his soul is elsewhere and, in this directed journey, reports back
every feeling. I do not leave the psychic voyager for longer than a
minute. But I know that in true Initiation, not this nursery flight, he
would be quite alone, with no reassuring voice.

There comes a pause. All has been pleasant up to now, as he has
described his walk through meadows and groves. But he mentions
that the terrain is becoming less verdant, the trees scarcer. The land,
he says, is waste. Then comes silence. And the silence is oppressive.

As I paused in my own notes, I project into his mind as far as I
can. "What is wrong?" I ask.

"It's a dragon," he says.

I do not laugh. After all, a dragon even about as quarter as real
as everyday life must be alarming.

"I can go no further", says the man, definitely.

Now I have to make a decision. Shall I bring him back to consciousness of the library? But in this case he would fail his self-appointed test. And he had asked for my assistance because he had failed himself in just such a test previously; and had bitterly regretted this ever since. So I try to remember what big game hunters do on such occasions.

I say, "Look at the dragon straight in the eyes!".

Though I have faith in my own inspired advice, on this occasion it is not at all successful. Quite the reverse.

"That is much worse," says Roderick. "His eyes are like car head-lights".

"Is this dragon going to attack you?"

"Oh no. He just won't let me pass him. When I go to the left, he is to the left. When I try to get round him on the right, he goes there. I can't get by. It is this dragon that made the land waste". I feel that we may sit here for hours unless something is done. In fact, Roderick seems quite pleased in a gloomy sort of way at being held by a dragon. I do not like to suggest his attacking the beast with a sword, for a particular reason. A few days ago our family had had an argument with Roderick over the value of the life of wasps. He regarded it as his duty to kill any who crossed his path. We always rescued any trapped in the house. In fact a day or so ago when Roderick had been helping my nephew make a bridge, they had disturbed a wasps' nest. The furious insects had left my nephew alone; but chased Roderick across a field and round the garden, much to the heartless pleasure of my young nieces. I could hardly, then, suggest a St. George attitude to this mammoth reptile. In our group opinion, dragons were as valuable in their own way as knights. One suspected some of us preferred them.

Romantically, I invent a spiritual solution.

"How about flying over the dragon?" I suggest, pleased with the symbolism. The soul must grow its wings.

"No," says Roderick. "I can't. Anyway I don't want to."

There is another silence, but this time a pleasant, creative one. Roderick is clearly very active, though not a muscle of his earthly body moves; not even an eyelid quivers. Then:

"I've done it!" he says with enormous satisfaction. "I've got by!

I crawled under him".

I felt this a most undignified way of dealing with a dragon; but have to accept this, as it is what he wants.

"What is happening now?" I ask.

"Funny," says Roderick. "I've found a wand. I'm pointing it at the withered grass and plants, and they are all growing!"

Still I want to know what the vision is all about.

"Ask what the dragon symbolizes", I say.

There is a wait while Roderick asks some invisible Helper. Then: "I am given to understand that the dragon typifies Inertia".

Now I feel that I can start bringing Roderick back. But I cannot leave the dragon unaccounted for. These things lurk in memory unless truly understood.

"Look back," I say. "What is the dragon doing now?"

Roderick reports in a puzzled voice: "There is no dragon... Ah! I see his empty skin! Yes - and now I see the fiery spirit of the dragon rising high into the air! This soul, having found its freedom, is rising to dangerous heights in the first intoxication of release!"

And this one episode of a trance experience well illustrates the joys and perils of exploring the depths of inner space. Roderick and I had twenty-six sessions together. He began trance vision finding himself an unborn baby in a cave, gazing upwards through an aperture at his sun-sign, Gemini, the heavenly twins. After sundry ordeals - the Initiation of the Fisher-King, a joust with a black knight on a black horse, he won his spurs of knighthood and rode forth successfully out of our shared trance world - and more prosaically, out of the castle in a car down the avenue.

And all this work began because I learnt to help children change their nightmares into happy dreams.

Does it often occur to most people how important sleep is? How strange that we should be self-aware during the day, and totally lose consciousness at night in a mimic death! Life is short enough as it is. How wonderful if we could live as self-conscious beings both during the day and the night. Then, used to these nocturnal trips into the psychic sphere, we would be prepared for the great journey that every soul must make at life's end. Moreover, grief at the death of others would be softened. For how could we lament the death of a friend, when we might meet that very friend alive and well, during the hours of night, in the psychic sphere?

However, the gap between full waking consciousness and the total oblivion of midnight is too great. Strive as one may, one cannot penetrate the veil of sleep and reach through to the sphere we call 'the unconscious'. But is it forever unconscious? When one wishes to move from one phase of awareness to another, the wisest course is to examine the intersecting zone where two levels meet. And this is the world of dreams. Dreams form the many-coloured veil that separates the psychic realm from our own physical existence. Appearing to be a kaleidoscope of jumbled nonsense yet, when the jigsaw is pieced together, another sort of sense is revealed that has the strange attraction of Edward Lear's 'Land where the Jumblies Live'.

When I had studied my own psychic experiences, I decided that control of that sphere could most easily be attained through dealing with dreams. For, I reasoned, if the first step to spiritual develop-ment came from controlling the emotions, it was extremely difficult to do this during physical life. This could lead to unhealthy suppression. The best place to deal with the emotions was on that level from whence they sprang - 'the Unconscious.'

Much emphasis has been placed upon the will in controlling feelings. This is the path of power. The mind uses the will in commanding 'lower self' to obey. However, in coping with the magical world of psyche, one learns that the last thing the soul will take any notice of is a command! Like water, the cunning desires find their own subtle way to circumvent rules and orders. And what is not permitted in waking hours will find expression in nightmares, expressing desire-fulfilment fantasies abhorrent to the waking mind.

The way round this, for me, anyway, was to realise that the psychic world was indeed the Land of Heart's Desire, and that only perverted and denied desires assumed an unhealthy expression. This realization for me sprang from faith that reality itself was harmonious and good; and so all that existed in mind and feeling had its own fulfilment in its appropriate sphere.

Therefore I had to discover what I myself really and truly desired. Not a vague aspiration or sense of duty; not instinct; but what I really desired with all my mind and heart. This required some courage, because I might have really and truly have wanted some-thing bad! But I did not. What I really found I wanted was love and beauty and truth. And I felt that so did everybody else, and so did animals and flowers and every being that existed.

Now this gave me the key to dream control. For I was not, by using my mind and will, forcing my soul to give up anything it genuinely wanted. Rather was I allowing it freedom to express its true nature. One has, in a sense, to coax one's soul into enjoying itself, to choose what it really likes. Hence it has to learn to say 'no' to what it does not truly want. And it does not like nightmares! But this exclusion of the unwanted, the irrelevant, need not condemn that which is rejected. For in a dream if one condemns the apparently unpleasing, one may be condemning oneself! The dragon in such a case is given an alarming reality. By killing the dragon or exorcising a demon, one may really be cutting off a part of one's own consciousness. And though such a drastic operation may in some cases be necessary, nonetheless one is left mutilated. It is best to find out what the dragon or demon symbolizes - what it has to say. The demon may not be so bad after all . . .

The usual method in dream therapy is for the patient to describe his dreams to a psychiatrist, and have their psychological meaning explained to him. But in this way he is still 'the patient,' passive. He is not active within the sphere of the dream itself. He hopes, when he is cured, not to have any more nightmares. He still cannot control his dreams.

But I discovered that it is possible and interesting to change one's dreams nearer to the heart's desire. To do this one has to bring more of one's waking consciousness through, to impinge on the dream. And this is best done in the borderland of sleeping and waking, at dawn and at dusk. This is the time of hypnogogic and hypnopompic visions.

And, though I learnt this art when grown up, it is best achieved in childhood. With adults I induced trance, and the experiences were aided by my guidance and help. But with children I only had to advise them what to do during sleep, and they obtained the same effects on their own!

With the children in the Castle, the obvious first step towards curing night-time screaming was to have them sleep together. Nowadays the poor human animal is forced into an unwanted solitude at night, unnatural, especially in early years. A night-light and the company of other children is more humane, especially with the very sensitive.

Take the case of Deirdre. Her reason for yelling her head off in her little dark room was perfectly understandable when explained years later. She said that, up to about the age of eight, regularly every night a company of 'witches' stood about her bed! She could see them with her eyes open. They wore black pointed hoods and long cloaks and stood silently gazing down at her. She insisted that she was not asleep. They would only disappear when she screamed loudly enough to get a grown-up to come and turn on the light.

A similar series of experiences used to befall a friend of mine, Fiona, when about the same age, five or six. But her 'witches' were actively unpleasant, and used to pinch her in an excruciating manner! Again, very naturally, she used to scream. And again the grown-ups did not understand why she yelled. She did not try to explain.

My method of coping with this sort of thing was to accept perfectly calmly the nature of such visitations, without suggesting that the child was making it up, or was unhealthy, or should just forget about it. I would explain that the world of night was completely different from the world of day, but real in another way. So naturally it had different laws. But it was not an evil world. It just seemed so when one was not used to it. I said that as it had its own laws, one had best learn them.

The first rule was to remember one's dreams. The next, was to be ready with rules of behaviour. For instance, when one was chased in that world, it was quite useless - worse than useless- dangerous, to try and run away! For in that place the more one tried to run, the weaker one's legs became, the more boggy the ground. The proper way to travel there was to imagine where you would like to be - say up a tree if chased by a tiger - and then imagine oneself there. And there surely one would be. Children can imagine vividly, and find little difficulty in understanding this. They can easily remember these rules when they dream.

The next law was not to be afraid. And one is only afraid when one hates. And one is apt to hate when one is afraid. So it was a good rule to feel friendly and act politely to every creature one met in a nightmare, however horrific it might appear. It would then, by the rules of this odd place, turn into something most unexpected and wonderful.

Another curious law of the dream world was that when one sent out a call for help, a person would turn up. It was not quite fair to send out a call for help to some particular person, because this might be a grown-up crossing the road at night, who might be distracted and get run over! The most important law of all was that in that night world people talked by thought-feeling. And they did things and made things by imagining. Ah! But there was a more important law! In this mysterious world, much more clearly than on earth, there were no accidents. As in fairy stories, if you behaved it would be nice. If you did wrong - it would be very nasty indeed. And then the only remedy was to say you were sorry at once, and not to do it again.

In this transmutation of the distorted and unpleasant into what the heart truly desires, I myself like the true meaning of the Nightmare. She is a small white horse who sits in a nest made of tree branches. Like the pouka of Ireland, if misused she can carry one over a precipice. But if loved and appreciated, she may grow the wings of Pegasus and carry one to the stars.

*'Made of Crystallized white light'*

# CHAPTER 3

# INHABITANTS OF THE PSYCHIC SPHERE

A WOMAN stood before me. I was wide awake. Her body seemed to be made of crystallized white light. Her hair was raven-black and pulled neatly into small dark curls. About it was tied a white veil, the ends hanging loosely. Her form was smooth, and her arms bare and roundly shaped. As for her dress, this intrigued me, for it appeared to be without any seams, although it was made up of strips of pale green and lilac material. I noticed the strong white shoulders. In fact shoulder, neck and arms gave an impression of concealed strength. But what struck me most forcibly was her way of speaking, which was through thought, but as clear as a musical instrument. What she said was:

"It is customary to stand in my presence."

Whereupon, rather crossly because it was snowy weather and night-time, I got out of bed and pulled on my red cardigan. Afterwards, when trying to describe The Lady, I said that she was a mixture of a Queen and a dancer and a gym mistress! I had seen television pictures of an earthly Queen's way of walking. But also this lady had the movement of a ballet dancer, as if she were balancing on a tightrope. But there was beneath the smooth silvery skin the feeling of the strength of an athlete. This reminded me of photographs of a Yogini.

Above all I instantly knew that I was in the presence of a goddess or an Angel, because of the power of her concentrated thought. Miserably I tried to control my own thoughts, which, at this important moment, out of sheer nerves came out with a stupid joke.

But the Lady took no notice of this. It was some silly joke about her smile, which I vaguely gathered was famous. She sat down on a chair facing my bed, her arms folded. And I sat facing her on the edge of my bed. And this lasted in total physical silence for at least half an hour. In her presence at last I was able to control my irrelevant thoughts. But the strange thing was that though I remember she spoke to me, I cannot recollect one word of what she said. And still, try as I may, there is nothing remaining that I can recollect. Finally, at the end of our interview, the Lady rose to her feet. Again I noticed the curious powerful yet beautiful way in which she moved. Shakespeare in The Tempest mentions Juno's majestic gait. This walk was unearthly, beyond human. Yet I felt that the Lady had once been human and had transcended this state.

Now comes a puzzling part. With spirits it is generally inferred that they appear, and then their visitation concluded, dematerialize. But I gathered from telepathy that this Lady had to wait for what I gathered was some sort of aeroplane. I remember vaguely wondering was it an Aer Lingus plane? Why should a Spirit need a vehicle? Stranger still, I had a very strong impression that this aeroplane would take her to a huge ship as big as the Queen Mary or bigger, that sailed high in the sky.

Anyway the Lady turned her back on me, and, curiously, as she moved away, her powerful neck muscles and her way of walking, rather like a lioness, reminded me of my childhood dream of the young man by the mosaic-paved fountain. She left through the window. I looked up at the dark sky but saw no aeroplane. The Lady, Goddess though she might be, appeared to have to wait! She was below me in the garden and sat on a parapet waiting, in the same attitude in which she had spoken with me, hands folded on her lap. She sat, a silvery figure surrounded by snow that gleamed in moonlight. I thought she must be feeling very cold in her evening dress. I waited for a long time, walking round and round my room. Each time I looked out, that still figure was seated in the garden, white veil over her black wavy hair. There was no sign of an aeroplane. Finally when I looked out, she had disappeared. I assumed she was travelling to her mysterious destination; so I took off my jersey, climbed into bed and, strangely enough in the circumstances, fell heavily asleep.

Such an experience brings one over the threshold of belief into knowledge. Yet the knowledge that beings exist beyond the physical world is not as yet provable in a scientific manner. At the time I realized this, for I myself was of a sceptical turn of mind, and knew well how deceptive the psychic sense can be. I can only say, as so many thousands of other people do, that I knew that the Lady was as real as myself and not an hallucination. I longed to tell people about her, and wondered how to do so.

The only way I hoped to achieve this without being laughed at or called deluded was to weave the experience into one of my novels. So I described a similar visitation in my fantastic novel: 'The Golden Eye'. But even so, I made it a dream, and because I thought the aeroplane and great sky ship too extraordinary, I left that part out. One of my friends said she always knew when I was introducing a psychic experience into one of my novels by my embarrassed way of writing.

It was only when I was in a railway carriage reading a copy of the now defunct magazine 'Everybody's', that I was amazed to see an artist's impression of a giant spaceship that had been seen by someone else. Up to then I had not paid much heed to Flying Saucer reports. Even so, I left the magazine behind me in the carriage, as I felt I was quite eccentric enough already, without believing in Flying Saucers! I notice this attitude among other pioneers of strange levels of consciousness. When at last I did join an Unidentified Flying Object Association, I was amused to observe that those who believed in physical spaceships from other planets did not care for their movement to be associated with 'the psychic lunatic fringe'. And psychics regarded the physical spaceship believers as naive materialists, bent on transforming psychic phenomena into schoolboy science fiction.

For myself, I have learnt to treat other people's experiences with respect, however unlike my own. No visionary can demand belief, but he can ask that his ultra-mundane reports be regarded as hypotheses. For it is unscientific to deny the existence of that which up to now is merely unproven.

Scientists and others who have all their knowledge from the realm of day, have only one key to the mystery of the Universe. But there are those who have earned the black key of the sphere of the night. And they too have their occult knowledge. To hold the keys of heaven and hell is not to bind and loose other souls: it is to control one's own consciousness not only in the material world; but also, like Psyche, to penetrate safely 'the Unconscious'.

To Psyche, guided by divine love, both realms became open. The Goddess Persephone is Daughter of Heaven and Queen of Hades. She combines the Outer and Inner, and holds the Crossed Keys on her breast.

Control then is the watchword of the lunar sphere. Emotional control. So may one successfully carry a cup of the Water of Life from the Well at the World's End, and bring it to those who need soul healing. Therefore sporadic spirit visitations are not enough. In such cases the inhabitants of other spheres visit us. But we ourselves must, if we wish to follow the path of the Mysteries, ourselves learn how to use our innate gifts.

In my case I decided to study the matter systematically. I had received visitations in full consciousness, that had convinced me that there were beings other than humans in the cosmos. And that we ourselves survived bodily death. But naturally I wanted to understand with my intellect, and also to control psychic manifestations. I did not want to be merely passive, relying solely on aspiration and prayer. In that way I was purely a receiver, a passive medium, however exalted might be visitors from spheres of light. Besides, I wanted to help those spirits whom I knew to be in trouble. So I went to the London College of Psychic Studies and started in a beginner's class with a famous medium, who specialized in working with scientists in England and the United States.

Here I discovered that, as in learning to drive a car, one is taught to stop the car first! People with psychic gifts frequently imagine that they should be opened up to the other world at any time. Also that they must receive any messages given and act on them! And many have the dangerous delusion that a mentor from the next world must, if he says so, be a Master, and so should be implicitly obeyed. Even in mediumistic circles, where control of the right of entry is understood, and the psychic beginners are taught to tune in and off at their own choice, Guides have possibly too much influence. I suppose this springs from centuries of religious faith, where faith accepts nor questions how. I think faith might well ask 'why?' For in this age of higher education and freedom of thought, the reign of the autocratic Master, whether Western Adept or Eastern Guru, is waning. The time of group participation, of spiritual democracy, is dawning.

The word for God in the beginning of the Bible is translated from the Hebrew word 'Elohim', a plural word that should therefore be correctly translated in the plural. It is not a masculine word either. The Pantheon of Heaven is beginning to be reflected on a world-wide scale by the springing up of meditation and psychic groups that work with blended group consciousness. It is humanity's first tentative step towards regulated telepathic communication.

The method follows much the same pattern, whatever the religious background of the group. Some form of invocation is used to deity whether called God, The Great Spirit or the The Truth. In circles using Eastern practice the 'tuning in' is brought about by the use of sound, or mantra. The group focuses its awareness by intoning some specific note. In Western circles, colour visualization is often used. The participants of the circle are asked to imagine a colour, or simply Light. This stills the restless mind, and also acts as a protection against unwanted thought-forms. One can pick up telepathically another person's worry just as easily as one can contract influenza!

Communication with a spirit in a very real way is still rare. I learnt to practice this safely during seances at the Spiritualist Association of Great Britain, in London. I also participated in their healing circles. The teacher of our class would say, if this were so, there would be no dubiety about proof, or difficulty of identification. The spirit could appear, say who it was, give all necessary information, including its previous earth address, and also easily satisfy a scientific researcher as to its objective reality.

As far as I know - and I have not as yet, alas, met a circle of illuminati who really can perform miracles on demand - we humans are at the very beginning of the development of our psychic faculties. Although Masters and Saints of our various religions so often had theurgic powers, their followers not only seem unable to do such miracles themselves, but, like the fox and the grapes, solemnly warn the faithful to avoid those very wonders which they themselves are incapable of doing.

So I found, studying in various classes, spiritualist and esoteric, that the most reliable method for contacting the unseen was by using symbols through eidetic imagery. Putting it simply, in one's mind's eye trained for the purpose, one saw projected a series of images connected with a chosen subject. In spiritualist circles, one usually had one's own alphabet of symbols: a ring for a marriage, a cake for a birthday, a series of associated images familiar to one's Guide and oneself.

As my sister-in-law, Valentine, complained, mediums saw things in bits; Aunt Betsy showing her umbrella, Uncle Tim his clerical collar, and the Guide, a pair of mocassins!

Occultists, I found, had their own group series of symbols handed down traditionally. Join an occult group, and you may learn to visualize the symbolism of the Tree of Life with its vividly coloured spheres. You can learn to visualize alchemical symbols, zodiacal signs and the incredibly complex Enochian hieroglyphs. This forms a language of communication for an Order and its guardian angels. The tattvic symbols of the elements do the same service for Eastern Oriented groups. Symbols are the language of the Unconscious.

In this way I learnt to use my own system of mental impressions well enough to demonstrate clairvoyance on television. This happened ten years after I had begun studying these subjects in London, and eleven years after we had opened the Castle as a semi-private Centre for Meditation and Study. A girl rang me up from Dublin and asked would I demonstrate as a medium on Irish television. I answered at once, no. One did not do that sort of thing publicly. "Why not?" asked the girl.

I could not give a satisfactory reply. I knew that professional mediums were willing to demonstrate publicly; but I still had a feeling that one must be private in one's psychic studies. Still, I was not a member of any secret society. Did I not want to share the good news that there was no death? I thought of a more cogent objection.

"They make such fools of spiritualists and psychic workers on television," I said. "You know, witches skipping around naked with background music of Teddy-bears' picnic! And the medium giving a sitting, and a patronizing announcer making fun - and a psychiatrist explaining that she is deluded, and a clergyman explaining that this sort of thing is un-Christian. Though why I don't know, considering the amount of spirits of various sorts that are described in the Bible.

Anyway, what would our neighbours think?"

But the girl said that Irish Television was unbiased, and that they would not 'send us up'; and that anyway she would be the interviewer. I thought she would be fair, and agreed, having asked the rest of the family, as they sat, arguing as usual, round the lunch table!

We had a glorious time when the television crew arrived. It was very sunny. Valentine would not join in, but sat on the window-sill watching, while we had lunch in the glare of lights while we were filmed. She said she had the eerie feeling that we ourselves were spirits, lighted into an unnatural whiteness. We were meant to be eating lunch in a usual way, discussing the family ghosts. It was hard to appear simple and natural with cameras focussed upon us, but after a few minutes it became natural. And I thought represented ordinary humanity eating lunch. Yet to Valentine, out of the picture, we looked like ghosts. We were deliberately ignoring the camera men, who in their turn were directing our behaviour, like guides or gods. And all this show was being done for nonexistent beings hoped for yet not yet manifest, called The Viewers. Surely the Viewers were real? As Viewers, no, not yet. The film might not prove acceptable; we might not appear.

Added to this over-lapping of spheres were the ancestors. They were being filmed, or rather their portraits, in old gilded frames. Two hundred years ago a lady with thick auburn hair and deep blue eyes, Barbara St. Leger, sat for her portrait in white fichu and blue gown. A short while ago a medium in London had described her, as still interested in us, her descendants.

And now we were trying to bring through our impressions of these spirit people whom we believed still existed on another level, to the attention of possible future Viewers. And we were being aided by the camera men and the interviewer. My nephew Finn was describing his experience of etheric projection . . .

"I was sleeping on the library couch," he said, "I woke up — I was completely awake, and I saw a monk, a handsome man, in dark robes standing at the foot of the couch. There was an elderly woman whom I could not see that I felt was behind me. They pulled me out of my body. It felt completely real. I really was outside my body which was lying beneath me. Then I came back and the monk and the lady had gone."

After this my brother Alexander was shown by the cameras playing on the organ in his Temple of Isis. They showed Finn's carved wooden figure of the Madonna of the Aquarian Age.

As an odd link with my interview with the Silver Lady, I had an impression of a lesser sort when I gave my clairvoyant demonstration to the interviewer. I chose our ruined abbey open to the evening sky, and filled with flowering shrubs. I had intended to stick to a simple demonstration of survival - but instead something else occurred. This was not a full psychic experience, but only a mental impression.

"I feel a presence", I said. "Now this figure is robed in white. She has got the most beautiful face. And, oddly enough, she is smaller than life-size. I see her like that, as if she were a little bit smaller, and yet real. Like a real statue. And she's holding - I'm getting shivers - you know the shivers one gets - She's holding a lovely golden cross. Now she is moving behind you. I feel she is guide and helper, that is, those people who come to us . . . now I mustn't talk too much - I must tune in again.

She says that we have been drawn together here, that in the country of Ireland there has always been a beautiful relationship with the world of spirit, that has never been blasphemed by killing people. That is, people didn't burn people for seeing nature spirits, and that the Angels are nearer here because Ireland has been cut off through misfortune, which is really a blessing. I am given to understand that you have been thinking about this - why misfortunes happen. And I am to tell you that life is like a school. People learn from experience."

I gave some personal messages and ended by saying: "There has been a lovely atmosphere of harmony: especially as this particular evening is Midsummer's Eve."

As I spoke these words, the camera photographed the ruined abbey window with its ivy and small statuette of Demeter. And the birds obligingly were singing. And I felt happy that at last, though feeling very shy and inadequate, I had given people a fleeting impression that had the beauty of my experience many years before of the Silver Lady, whom I associated with the moon. As for that small white-robed figure, I have no name to give her. But I rather hope she was a woman of the Sidhe - our Irish Faery People.

# CHAPTER 4

# RESCUE WORK

IN her sitting-room in London, leaning back in an armchair, lay my friend Marie. She was in a trance. In her case there was no need for me to induce trance through suggestion. All I had to do was to say a prayer, and to formulate our intention. For it is not enough to have good intention; one needs to express clearly what one wishes to do. In this case Marie wished to use her natural gift of trance. Up to now, there had been men who had tried to exploit her gift, so she had given up any adventures into the world of the unseen. But not to use a gift is to feel frustrated, restless. And I knew that there could be much good work for her to do in the way of healing and psychic therapy. For disembodied spirits needs psycho-therapy as much as those in physical bodies. Often more so.

Marie had entered trance quickly. Now she began to display agitation, and reported that she found herself inside an aeroplane. And she knew that this plane was going to crash. I asked her for more identification, but she said that she could not understand the passengers' language. Her attention was focussed on a small girl with fair pig-tails. This girl was with her parents. Marie said she was trying to communicate with the parents, but without success. However, she said that the child was aware of her presence.

Now Marie became so upset that I wondered should I encourage her to return from trance. She kept repeating that the plane was running into fog, and that it was going to crash. She mentioned ice forming on the wings. I realized that she was so fearful of impending disaster, that I must bring her out of the plane at once. So I told her to leave before the crash, and bring any passengers she could contact with her. Here was the use of directed trance, and the ability to build scenes. I described a garden, and told Marie to shut her eyes, and imagine she was in the garden. There was a pause and she said she was there. I asked her to open her eyes and describe the garden. I did this because I wanted to make sure she was located in consciousness out of harm's way. She described a simple English style garden which sounded pleasantly suburban. Then came the important part. I said could she see any passengers from the crashing plane? She replied that the little girl was with her in the garden. The child was in a great state of distress at losing her doll. It had been left in the aeroplane. Marie could not comfort her.

Remembering the rules of dream world, which I felt also applied to this psychic realm, I suggested that Marie would find the doll in the garden - but first I asked her to get a description of it from the little girl. For teleportation in this sphere was, I knew, accomplished through visualization, and an effort of the will. There was a wait while Marie searched. Then, triumphantly, she declared that she had found the doll lying among some bushes!

I felt that she had been in trance long enough. For I always timed sessions according to arrangement with the Sensitive. But what should we do about the little girl? For somewhere, at some time, I believed that this plane crash had reality. And so the child's plight mattered. I asked Marie to send out a strong mental call for help. I joined her in this. I said that a Helper would come.

As is so often the case, the Helper was not a romantic looking Guide in flowing robes - but someone perfectly prosaic.

'A nurse is coming into the garden by the gate,' said Marie. 'She is very brisk and efficient. I don't like the bossy way she's talking to the little girl. Surely she should be more sympathetic? She is re-tying her pig-tails, and she's saying: "That doll needs a good wash". Clearly Marie felt that 'the newly dead' should be addressed with more respect: but I was used to nurses, and knew that their hard commonsense helped far more than sentiment in a crisis.

Marie gave the nurse's name and that of her hospital. "She says when she was on our side she was a sister in this Liverpool hospital"; explained Marie. "She says they ran out of penicillin there during the war. Now she is taking the little girl away with her

.... I wondered what happened to her father and mother?"

I said firmly that it was time for Marie to return to everyday life. Afterwards I asked her what the degree of reality had been in comparison with everyday life. She replied that she felt that she had really been in that plane. Consciousness of her physical body on the armchair had completely disappeared. In fact she kept repeating that if she had stayed in the plane she would have been killed with all the passengers! I had to repeat more than once that her body had been sitting in the armchair all the time, and that she had been reporting back to me.

For this is a story of dual consciousness. How could Marie report coherently to me, her body in an armchair in London, while she herself believed that she had been in an aeroplane? One can see how hard it would be for an observer to make out which of us was speaking the truth, if we were to tell our stories separately.

The only way a psychic experience of such actuality can be identified as such, and not confused with the physical, is when the psychic herself, as in this case, knows that she is in trance. In fact, I like the joke of one spirit saying to another: "Do you believe in life before death?"

The only way one can understand multi-consciousness is to realize that our experience of the five senses is only a fraction of total consciousness. And that psychic awareness is also only a fragment of the totality of what we truly are. Schizophrenia is not merely a disease of some, but the endemic state of the entire human race! We only see in reflection a part of our real selves.

So 'Rescue Work' is really the identification of fragmented parts of people's souls, and trying to co-ordinate the part in harmony with the whole. The task is to find the unhappy dreamer and help him to wake into happiness. Indeed one could say, from a metaphysical point of view, that all physical life on earth is a form of related group dreaming. Each individual has the limitation of 'self', and finds himself forced to have relationship with the other dreamers. Seldom does the dreamer awaken. For the very doors of a higher reality are barred to him by the oblivion called sleep. And the psychic plane too may be regarded as an area of group dreaming; but on a more conscious and so on a greater scale.

As the greater contains, and so controls, the lesser, so therefore power over conditions of the psychic area gives also control of physical life. Disease and psychosomatic disturbance are best cured from the inner plane of the emotional life of the soul. And emotional control itself is brought about by the use of mind. The kind of mind that learns to use the psychic faculty is best understood as a creative union of reason and will. The power it uses is that which we underrate as 'imagination'. For what is art - painting, music, sculpture - but an expression of the awareness of the soul of that reality behind our dreaming earth life?

There are those occultists who wish to side-track the psychic level; and mystics who prefer to ascend in consciousness straight up to the cosmic level of Spirit, ignoring the intervening level of the psyche. This is the path of the Master Builder whom Ibsen describes as ascending a church spire, which he has caused to be built, until he has attained the very top. But the fate of the Master Builder was that he fell off! This fall in the play is - as so often - attributed to Woman. There are the three aspects of Eve in the play: the meek follower who obeys, the dominating wife, and the ideal daughter figure. The meek follower bores him; the wife wants to put him in a mental home; and the 'ideal daughter' eggs him on to the heights. But she is the one who destroys him by waving a white scarf in his honour - like that White Feather distributed to men by patriotic females in the First World War, egging them on to kill. Distracted by her enthusiastic waving of the white scarf - in the height of his triumph - he falls.

So may the aspiring spiritual climber, pursuing the goal of becoming Adept, a Master, fail. His symbol is the Tarot card of two figures falling from the window of a tower which, struck by lightning, itself tumbles to the ground. One can imagine a planet itself torn apart by unbalanced use of the will by those aspiring to the heights.

The answer to such a problem would appear to lie in the mysterious words I once heard, but could not then understand: 'None may reach Christ save through Mary'. Or, as I was given from the world of Spirit: 'One must approach Truth with courage: Love through humility'. The Initiation of Water, of the good use of the emotion, must be undertaken before the Initiation of Fire, the use of the intellectual will. And, in many Western traditions, Woman represents the lunar or psychic sphere of the soul.

Truly one is asked by the presiding Powers to enjoy, not to deny, one's soul. And the soul's essence lies in true individuality, in which exists the spark of divinity within each being. Not a snowflake is like another. It is in difference that lies the pleasure of harmony of the whole. If anything or any being were an exact replica of another - it would not exist! It would be a mere reflection.

It seems strange that anyone should have to defend the psychic sphere and the psychic faculties. But the dualistic teaching of a divided Divinity, of two forces, Dark against

Light, has given anyone exploring the metaphysical consciousness a fear of 'the astral'. Astral means starry, and I do not care for a euphemism that refers to 'the lower astral'. It sounds like cold cream for sore feet! But perhaps well describes that disapproving attitude of the righteous when facing the whole sphere of spiritualism, psychic research and parapsychology.

If I were to give one word that expresses the essential importance of the psychic or 'astral' sphere, I would say Beauty. How repellent is the Do-Gooder, the Intellectual, the Spiritual Climber, without beauty! For beauty does not have to push and climb, need not seek to out-strip others, nor denigrate rivals, and does not have to look to some future end. For Beauty already has attained, already exists in The Now. And, above all, is loved by every living thing. Hence it has perfect humility without knowing its own humility. Let us then enjoy 'the Astral' plane, as a perfect work of art, a pleasing play put on by Divinity for the mutual enjoyment that brings us into harmony with all other creatures. For the Master Builder was alone up there on his solitary spire. He had left those who loved him below on the ground . . . They survived him.

This humble harmony with all other creatures is particularly easy to enjoy in the psychic realm. For anthropomorphic statements that 'Man is Lord of Nature', 'Man is the most Advanced', 'Only he has the gift of speech', 'only Man has a soul', have no meaning in the psychic sphere. For in that world it is a fact that animals have souls, because there they are, having survived! And it is possible for us to communicate with them. And they can talk to each other. Alice found that, through the Looking-Glass, Tiger-Lilies talked to her. This was no fantasy, though told in a children's story. In the psychic world plants can talk in their own way. So they may do on this side but in the other world one can listen and even join in the conversation! For a greater level of awareness extends the limitations of one's self-consciousness: it overlaps into the consciousness of other beings. Sensitives see as many spirits of animals as humans, though these contacts are not so often recorded; for the simple reason that animal relatives on this side are not asking for communication! They seem to have it anyway - especially cats. Angela, who has a particular love for cats, gave me an interesting example of this. She was setting out for her London office, when to her horror she saw the body of a cat that had been run over, lying in the middle of the road. It was very dead. But she also saw clearly the spirit form of the cat beside its dead body. She said that the ghost cat could see her, and she persuaded it, though it was frightened, to come into her arms. Finally it settled on her shoulder, and she half expected someone would call attention to it! The cat remained with her all day at the office perching on her shoulder as she typed, and even went to lunch with her! As it showed no sign of leaving her, her problem was, would her own cat at home notice this supernatural guest, and object; which she would certainly do to an earth cat coming to stay.

Angela duly arrived home to her flat - and was left in no doubt as to the psychic faculties of her own cat. She hissed and arched her back, and made every effort to drive the unwelcome guest away. Angela felt like a smuggler of an illegal immigrant. She did not want to send the ghost cat away and sent out in thought a call for help. Suddenly appeared a tribe of spirit cats! Her ghost cat lost interest in Angela and decided to join the ghostly pack. And off they all streaked.

Those who live in the Castle develop an attunement with living nature. Valentine can physically communicate with plants and flowers. Curiously enough, she finds it more embarrassing to talk about this, than to describe seeing human spirits. Plant communication has the association of 'twee' children's stories, of 'Tinker-Bell', and of 'Feyness'. For all I know serious Professors, Brigadiers and School-mistresses may go into their gardens and have long conversations with trees and flowers; but rather naturally do not mention it. Only children of under seven are allowed to use 'the daffodil telephone'. It is certain Russian and American scientists now who are bringing this psychic faculty into good repute, by experiments suggesting that plants respond to our thoughts. Hundreds of people have known this all their lives.

I asked Valentine to tell me about her conversations, and what trees and plants were like in character. Was she certain she was not in actuality conversing with nature spirits tending the plants? She said she could communicate with nature spirits occasionally, but that she could converse directly with flowers and plants.

"I can't talk to the cultivated ones in the garden", she said.

"They don't talk to me, though perhaps they do among themselves. "It's the wild flowers that talk".

"In actual words?"

"I hear them in words. For instance, yesterday I heard a tiny little call coming to me from the end of a field. I was going in to lunch, but I had to find who was calling . . . She wanted to be looked at. Finally I found her, a tiny little dog-violet plant at the wild end of the hedge at the bottom of the field. Some flowers talk in verse. These ones are very moral; They like telling people to be good. The May Trees though are wild and gay and untidy. The dog-violets are more natural and jolly, and the purple ones are quite different and shy. Gorse bushes are proud and glorious.

"I did see a dog-violet fairy a short while ago. She wore a gown just like a flower, and she was saying something about being happy and how gloriously happy the spring is. How perfect everything is. I don't often see tree fairies. Last autumn though, in the wild wood, I saw a hazel-nut boy. He had curly brown hair and was very funny. He didn't really like people coming, but he said he liked the children gathering his nuts. But he mostly liked the red squirrels coming and taking his nuts. I haven't seen the squirrels, but I'm sure they come."

I guessed that Valentine could communicate with flowers easily on the earth plane because she lived very much in the present. She said she never even thought, let alone worried, when she went for a walk across the fields. She needed no arranged seance or meditations. She was part of nature herself.

And this is the secret of 'Rescue Work'. You rescue trees and flowers and people and animals from hurt because they are part of yourself. On the earth plane this is hard to realize. On the psychic level, harmony of all beings is a law which, when understood, gives one the freedom of that sphere.

# CHAPTER 5

# URANUS THE MAGICIAN

I WAS standing in the doorway of the Cafe of the Victoria and Albert Museum, looking around for a young man whom I had not met. Owen, having heard that I worked with people in trance, had asked to meet me. At first I had refused. Trance sessions took up so much of my time and energy, that I would only undertake them if I felt that there was genuine need, or some gift that needed developing. Owen, his friend had told me, wished to study the Western Tradition of the Mysteries, particularly the Arthurian Quest for the Holy Grail. She herself was following an Indian method of meditation with a group. She knew that I was willing to help people find their own particular path, as long as I felt it led to good. I was myself attracted to the Grael legend, so finally I agreed to meet Owen. I knew he was nineteen, but had no other description.

I chose my plates of food on a tray, and then examined the people at the various tables. My attention was attracted to one particular young man sitting bolt upright with a brief case by his side. He had neat short black hair, a white collar and dark suit. He seemed to be the only person waiting for someone. I thought, 'Oh no! Not him!' But put my tray down at his table.

Then I became aware of another young man approaching the table. He was slim and dark; he had the air of a gypsy, combined with that of a medieval troubadour. Yet there was nothing unusual about his clothes. We acknowledged each other at once.

I liked Owen. He had a pleasant personality, warm-hearted and romantic. In my mind I classified him according to the Knights of

65

the Round Table. This was not Percival, nor Kay nor Galahad. Something about him reminded me of a musical film 'Camelot'. He was Sir Launcelot! Owen was half French, half Welsh.

We arranged to do a series of sessions, beginning in our friend's flat in London and, if the preliminary efforts were promising, to continue them in Ireland.

During the first session I found that Owen could enter trance easily, though he had not done this sort of work before. His gift lay in seeing an astonishing range of symbols, expressed in colourful scenes. His weakness lay in his inability to hear or receive any telepathic thoughts. His mind was like a coloured film without a sound track. I noticed that this correlated with his personality. For Owen loved the world of nature, of visual impact; but found self-expression through thought and speech extremely difficult. In fact he told me that he had only read about two books on mysticism and the occult. He preferred to understand directly through symbols, without words. And, like Valentine, in consequence he had brilliant clairvoyance.

His two opening trance adventures showed me what his line of development was. And it was not Arthurian. It was Arabic. What interested me was that it seemed to be a pure and mysterious Arabic knowledge, that concerned itself with the cult of the Dove and the White Rose. In his early trance experiences he identified himself with a small dirty Arab boy with bare feet, though his earthly personality rejected this. He wished to be a Knight. Nor were his instructors those that he thought he wanted. Here were no Ladies with white pointed head-dresses, nor did the Sage who finally came to him have much resemblance to Merlin, though he hoped that this was so. And the teachings brought through were new for both of us. I had that glorious feeling 'the Operator' has when suddenly psychic contact with some hierarchy is established. We were 'through to our contacts', as occultists would put it.

Here one must examine what these contacts mean. For psychotherapy used to develop creative imagination may be acceptable to modern science, but not the existence of paranormal Teachers. This usually is regarded as unproven; at worst, hallucinatory. Nor can one prove the Great Ones' reality. One knows it oneself, and one shares the knowledge with others. One tries to work with the Great Ones. This is all one can do.

However there are certain pointers that enable one to check on the external validity of a Teacher. For one thing, someone in trance will answer from the subconscious a question put to him. Usually a hypnotized subject is asked the routine question: 'Were you happy at school?' 'What do you feel about your mother?' And the subject will try to answer truthfully. Psychiatrists don't usually ask questions such as: 'Have you a soul that survives death?' 'Do Angels exist?' Is there a God?' If they did, they might get surprising answers.

So I ask a person in trance questions about Teachers, and get what I feel to be a reasonable reply. And, when trance is finished, 'the percipient' is perfectly capable of giving a rational assessment of the degree of reality of the experience. Instead of the doctor and patient relationship, of hypnotist and subject, there is in the method I use, collaboration between two equals in a mutual experiment. The telepathic rapport of 'Operator' and 'Percipient' extends also to the Spirit Guide, whose mind blends with that of Operator and Percipient, each with individual choice and responsibility for the work in hand.

I have found that usually there is not one teacher, but a group. This gives a balanced scheme of teachings to those on earth receiving the messages; and a feeling of safety in numbers. The group teaching given to Owen and myself during these sessions were led by one calling himself 'The Sage'. As described by Owen, he was a white bearded man, wearing a purple cloak fastened by a crescent moon brooch. He bore a staff which he used in a curious way as a wand. With him were associated the Three Ladies. They first showed themselves to Owen separately; finally together in a cave.

The first was the Lady with red hair. Owen saw her in a woodland scene, wearing fifteenth-century costume. Her hair was bound with pearls, and her gown was full, and coloured yellow and blue. Owen's task was, with the aid of a gypsy, to bring her a bundle from a Roman villa with a mosaic patio. The symbolic head delineated in the centre of the mosiac pavement was that of a helmeted warrior. The bundle was given to the gypsy by an old woman. Owen finally brought it to the Lady in the wood.

The focal part of this experience was the nature of the contents of the bundle. Owen realized that this belonged to the Lady of the wood: not to the warrior. And when he untied the bundle he found two candlesticks, and a golden chalice with rubies. So his first session brought at once the Grael which he sought. And he had to give it away, though he had been tempted to keep it. The teaching given was thus conveyed, not in words, but in symbols.

The Grael he sought was not, as he has thought, within the jurisdiction of the Warrior King. Rather was he to seek for it among humble peasant women and gypsies, in the depths of woodlands. It seemed quite a good indication that he should come to Ireland!

The second Lady who instructed him was the Woman at the Well. She appeared when we began our Irish sessions in the library. She appeared to him as Moorish, her face veiled; and she gave him a drink of well-water in a pitcher. Her teachings concerned the alchemical transmutation of metals, and the animation of amulets through the co-operation of elemental spirits.

In a series of vivid dramas, she showed him the history of a scarab amulet from its creation by a goldsmith in Hittite times, through battles, seiges and robbery and recovery, to its present day hiding place in a cave, dusty and without its green stone. Again I felt that underlying the interest of the story and its alchemical implications, lay the philosophical point that Nature, represented by the emerald, had been trampled upon by armed men.

His third Lady was the most exalted. She was the Lady of the Doves. She appeared to him as a white-robed figure with great white wings, surrounded by doves. She presided over the Home of the doves. To her belonged the area of purification through the element of water.

But undoubtedly the dominating figure in all Owen's trance experiences was The Sage. The Sage's method of teaching was to use his staff and other 'physical' objects, and through them to convey his teachings. Indeed I wondered if this was how Teachers taught their disciples in the days when few could read or write. For the Sage's staff could obligingly become a serpent, a pointer, or a wand; his moon brooch the moon itself! It was hard work for us to get through these teachings. They would come during heaviest trance. Trances deepen through clearly defined stages. Owen's preliminary experience, Stage One, would begin in country surroundings, sometimes in France. The first Helper, whom Spiritualists call the Gate-Keeper, would show himself in the guise of a

Carter, a Horseman, or possibly a peasant gathering sticks. This reminded me of a fairy-tale etiquette, when the youngest prince treats a hunchback or an old crone with respect, and so is guided in his own quest. Owen's first guide would point the way silently down the path he was expected to follow.

Stage Two led to a deepening trance. The way of entry to the next scene was usually through darkness and limitation - and I was amused at the various ways in which Owen found his doorway! The doorway could be a tunnel, a pool, a dolmen, a looking-glass; and, once when he was in a room and I could see no way out for him, he went up the chimney!

It was in Stage Two world that he met the Ladies and had adventures set in historical periods and places - in medieval castles and forests. This was a world of emotional experiences of love and adventure, like a Walter Scott novel.

Stage Three was entered through still deeper trance, and it is here with many people that memory cannot be brought back. But Owen could remember. Stage Three was entered through the coming of light. Owen could see a star high in the sky, or simply light. He would ascend into this - and it was in this sphere of consciousness that he would meet the Sage. For this was a world of symbols, of fluctuating forms that each carried their enigmatic meaning. Here he learnt of suns and worlds.

The Sage's teachings about the lunar sphere were of great fascination for us, and I had not read of anything like these before. He would use ordinary objects to illustrate great meanings.

On one occasion he laid seven small stones on the desert sand. They were coloured red, yellow, green, blue, black, white and purple. The Sage pointed with his staff at the yellow stone and the white one. These became Sun and Moon in the sky, and the Sage's Violet mantle became Space. The point of the teaching was that there was an etheric 'rope' of connecting radiations linking earth to moon. This, Owen said, looked like a luminous white twisted rope from the outside, but was rainbow coloured within. He said that there were also these connecting 'ropes' of radiations connecting sun and earth, and sun and moon. In fact, seen in this psychic way, each coloured stone became a planet with connecting radiations, like a Maypole, with the planets merrily dancing round the central sun, linked with differing coloured ribbons!

But in the story we were given the situation was hardly merry. Repeatedly Owen was shown black clouds, presumably of pollution - either psychic or physical - upsetting the earth's balance. He was shown the 'rope' between the earth and the moon break. What was interesting was that finally it was the earth and not the moon that broke its connection with the sun, and flew off into outer space! The little moon took its place and took its turn as an independent planet, joining the maypole dance in orbit round the sun.

I notice that young people are quite happy about thoughts of a coming cataclysm. They like drama; and coping with cosmic disasters seems to promise more excitement than spending an incarnation working in an office! In this case I said that possibly these visions need not contain a physical prophecy, but might convey a symbolic meaning. Rejecting his soul sphere - the moon - man might also lose connection with the Spiritual Sun. Or, putting it personally, like most of us Owen needed to cope successfully with his emotional problems before he took on deeper esoteric work.

In these sessions I always brought Owen back slowly, stage by stage, in the way he had come. We would end with sending out Healing, then we would give our reports of what had happened, and our opinion as to what the visions were about.

When dealing with the subject of hypnotism, one is generally brought up against a very natural prejudice. There is the fear that 'the subject' is put under the will of some Svengali-like operator and, even if the subject cannot be made to do something against his spiritual will, still there is the suspicion that he has been subject to brain-washing, called politely 'suggestion'. After all, in other fields the same relationship applies: the teacher instructs the pupil; the priest teaches the faithful. How alarming is the thought of subjecting oneself to the influence of another human while one is in trance! It brings thoughts of interrogation by intelligence officers as depicted in television plays. As for a woman Operator, such Ladies are shown as very powerful - and therefore alarming, as in Bulwer Lytton's 'The Coming Race'. In this novel female 'Gy-ei' are portrayed as sending men into deep trance by a mere pointing of the finger at the gentlemen's brows!

Therefore in my work of inducing trance I do not use the word 'hypnotism'. 'Hypnos' means sleep, and the percipient in my method does not sleep. Next, I keep 'suggestion' to a minimum, and only give advice when asked. I start usually with 'building' an imaginary temple as safety precaution, for this temple gives the percipient a place of refuge that yet forms part of his trance. For the dreamer finds it hard to wake up at once in earth conditions. I bring him back to the temple at the end, and from there we send our thoughts of healing for others. But the intervening dreams are the individual choice of the percipient, who decides what to do, what to accept, and what to reject. Learning to do so in trance experience, he hopes to control his waking life in the same way. If in trance he can face a dragon with equanimity - even establish a friendly relationship with it; he hopes to cope more successfully with his employer, who has an odd dream resemblance to the dragon . . .

The most dramatic proof of one's own psychic development and control is the recognition in earthly flesh of the Spirit Master. Of course this Master may be a man or a woman. The pupil has been taught during sleep and trance state by a Master. He remembers these lessons. He knows the appearance of his Teacher perfectly. Then one day he goes to a meeting, or a dinner party, and, suddenly, in walks his Teacher in the flesh! And he knows that he is passing from the lunar sphere of psychism into the orbit of the Spiritual Sun. There is a change in his consciousness. He may expect to face his Initiation of the Purification of the Moon, before he can start again in a new school of undreamt of activity.

# CHAPTER 6

# INITIATION OF THE MOON

WE are seated in the library of the castle, in group meditation. Group meditation is more difficult, I have found, than directed trance. For in directed trance the psychic traveller is in constant touch with the Operator, and receives guidance. At any moment, if the experience becomes too much, he can be brought back. But some who have had successful trance experience find, when left to themselves in meditation, that unpleasant, even horrific visions can come to them, resembling waking nightmares.

And it is an ordeal for someone, untrained except through studying a few books, to sit alone and in silence, allowing hidden depths of consciousness to unfold. If some expansion of consciousness should occur, this can prove overwhelming.

A half-way stage between directed trance experience and solitary meditation, is group meditation. Here the travellers set forth together in shared imagining, concentrating on a chosen area for contemplation. Then comes the silence during which each individual treads his chosen path alone. But, at the end of a stipulated time, say ten minutes to half-an-hour, the leader of the group calls the wandering souls back. Symbolism is unravelled, and points of cross-reference discovered. It is diversity within a framework of unity.

When I lead a group, I describe the same imaginary Temple or garden that I use in individual work for one person. I invoke Deity, and ask for the aid of Helpers. I then describe as vividly as I can the chosen scene, and ask my fellows in the circle to imagine this themselves. Beyond the Temple or garden, I say, is a pleasant landscape. Here each person may go forth on his chosen path, seeking guidance and inspiration. As some may enter deep trance, I stipulate that at the end of a certain period of silence, my voice will call them back to the set scene, in which we will send forth healing thoughts for others.

It was in group meditation in the library that Fiona gave us her report of the Temple of the Moon. Our library is an oblong room, lined with books, and the furnishings are golden, light brown and green. It is on the second storey of the Castle, with a battlemented balcony overlooking a terrace, and the long sombre line of the yew walk. In the evenings, when we had our meditations, the shadow of the old part of the castle lay lengthily aslant the lawn; and the wood-pigeons and the rooks would call from their wilderness beyond the yew walk. The members of this particular group of sessions were Alexander, Valentine, Hari - an Indian Vedantist, Nicholas, and Fiona herself. Nicholas was taking his turn at being group leader, and so sat in the East, robed in white. However he did not remain there in Fiona's visions. In her first report she said Nicholas disappeared, and his place on the caned high-backed chair of honour was taken by a Moon Lady. This Lady had raven hair, silvery skin and wore a crescent Moon head-dress. The rest of us remained in her vision, and she assumed that Nicholas must be walking around outside somewhere. We were dressed, she said, in a mixture of Egyptian and late Graeco-Roman attire. She saw a strange young man as Gate-keeper at the Western door, who wore brown leather and held a sword. He knocked on the ground twice to begin proceedings.

My brother Alexander was facing the Lunar Priestess in the West by the door. He was dressed as an Egyptian, Fiona said, and held a staff with two points at the top. I was seated on the Lady's right, and was wearing a neat wreath of gilded leaves, and was busy writing notes. I did this in the earth library anyway! Valentine, Hari and herself were wearing Greek-style costume. We seemed to be an eclectic lot, rather as we were in daily life, I thought. I could imagine a liberal minded group of Graeco-Romans at the time of the decline of the Roman Empire, practising Egyptian-type rites in a pleasant temple attached to a white marble villa.

For the visionary Temple in which we sat was large and circular, according to Fiona, and was made of white marble. The floor was checked like a chess-board, black and white.

The Moon Priestess, during each vision, would first walk around the circle, sprinkling something like mica or powdered silver out of a little pot hanging at her waist. She would look at us as if to see how we were. Then we would group ourselves around a cauldron in the centre of the room, with a small fire burning in it. The Lady would sprinkle purple powder on to the little fire that made it spurt into flame. We would watch closely, waiting. At last, at the climax, from the fire would glide a golden serpent. The ritual would end as it had begun, with the Gate-keeper knocking on the ground, this time once.

None of us knew what this could be about; but we enjoyed the glamour of Fiona's description. I said that Fiona was building us a nice white Flying Saucer in the form of a band-box white Temple, and that we all took off in this for a psychic trip, duly returning in time for supper!

Particularly compelling were the later sessions in which Fiona reported that the scene was changing. I was reminded of my favourite 'Through the Looking-Glass,' when Alice began to move from one square to another. For some time Fiona had reported seeing a mysterious curtained door in the East. Later she had glimpses of a long dark passage . . .

As this resembled a shift into deeper trance of an individual percipient, I was aware that our whole group might well be entering another level of awareness. Instead of the usual silent Gate-keeper Guide, Fiona reported seeing a mysterious bird. He was snowy white, she said, with a golden beak and golden legs.

In our final session, she found herself in the dark passage and, through a narrow window, she had a glimpse of the Priestess of the Moon sailing away in a long black boat on a deep blue sea. She was rowed by bronze-coloured men with gold head-bands, like Egyptians. The Priestess raised a white arm in salutation. We had left the Temple of the Moon.

It was only after many years that I realized that we ourselves in that group had moved from our preoccupation with the psychic world, into the more intellectual sphere of the Occult. From passive mediumistic experience we were moving into a more active participation in the esoteric field.

Yes, but had we successfully passed a lunar initiation? For not one of the three Worlds, the physical, the psychic and the spiritual is more important than the other. Man has a tripartite being, body, soul and spirit, and a weakening of one of these leads to unbalance, even a fall back into an earlier stage. For a person can be successfully developed in one sphere, have a brilliant intellect - and yet be lamentably deficient in emotion. Yet emotion well used is the fuel power of the will.

Another sort of unbalance manifests in an emotional person who lives in a Wagnerian state of turbulent passion, without the controlling power of the mind. As for a lack of artistic appreciation in someone otherwise clever and feeling, this can lead to such unattractiveness that the person can even make goodness and knowledge seem boring.

Of course each individual takes life's initiations in a different way, and in different order. A tidy way is to control the emotions by the mind, and from there develop cosmic consciousness. In my own case I began with mystical experience and from there I tried to interpret through the 'sun level' of the mind; and finally realized the extreme importance of the emotional 'astral' sphere of the moon.

The final result must be the same: in one's own unique way to synthesize the three worlds within oneself and from thence to relate successfully to all those whose lives in any way touch one's own, whether human or animal, plant or the elements themselves.

Nonetheless, although many prefer to start with the Spirit or with the mind, most people with whom I have have worked feel that they cannot deal with either of these states, without first dealing with their feelings. And, when in trance, this takes the form of a birth experience through the element of water.

I have not observed the need for birth experience in women percipients; but each man I worked with, young or middle-aged, found himself as a small boy in his beginning trance experiences. The little boy would be poor and dirty and lost. At first when this happened I thought it might be a case of reincarnation. But the subsequent adventures were so clearly natal, that I had to face the fact that these men were bent on being born again in a more satisfactory manner!

To take the experience of Owen. Having begun as the poor Arab boy and grown into a youth, guided by the Lady of the Water-jar, suddenly in one of our sessions he began a new trend. It was the Lady of the Doves who for him brought Ordeal by the element of water; though for him the ordeal was not very unpleasant. He found himself as a youth standing by a pool, and the Lady of the Doves was facing him across the water. She told him to undress and bathe in the pool. As he was modern in outlook, Owen was puzzled by the action of the Lady as he undressed and stood naked. She covered her face with her great white wings - and I felt here the Moorish influence of the veiled face. Perhaps the gesture had a deeper symbolism. Then Owen entered the pool . . .

Now I could feel, as he lay on the library couch, that Owen was entering into a deeper state of trance. There was the usual altered rate of breathing. At these times I myself had a curious feeling of dual consciousness, as if I were not only sitting in the darkened room with my notebook, but was also projected into the trance vision, helping to shape and guide if need be.

"I've got right under the water!" said Owen. "I've gone through the bottom of the earth. Now I am crawling down a very narrow black tunnel. It is very narrow. I can hardly move. But I've got to move on. Strange . . . I have become a baby."

He seemed in no particular discomfort but was concentrating intently on his struggles. I waited patiently. Both of us were puzzled. I did not see why Owen had to turn into a baby, just when he had grown from the little Arab into a young man. I was used to people going down long dark passages, but this seemed more like the heavy and dangerous task of a coal-miner burrowing into the earth. I wondered what Owen was up to, and whether to help. But he seemed determined to press on unassisted. Then he suddenly cried:

"I see the Light."

I was relieved. I was thinking of mundane time, of supper! There was silence; then he said:

"I'm looking out from the mouth of a cave. I'm looking down on a lot of people. They look like early Druids or something like that. The men have long grey beards and wear white robes, and the women have long garments. What they are doing is to hail the four quarters. They are turning to each quarter in turn to hail the sun; and I am afraid that when they turn in my direction, they may see that I am spying on them. I am afraid of falling . . ."

It was strange that though Owen lay rigid in trance I felt that exciting things were happening to him. Then:

"I fell right down from the tunnel into a cave." He said.

"I tumbled down into the midst of them, but they are not angry. They have picked me up. It's all right. They are examining me . . ."

And so through the mediatorship of the Lady of the Doves, Owen felt himself reborn into the world of the Ancients. From then on he continued his adventures as an adult, still faithful to his earliest intention of seeking the Holy Grael. But I felt that already he had psychologically achieved the Cup of Water. He did not again find himself as an unsure boy.

The final apotheosis of Owen's lunar initiation was the coordination of the three aspects of Eve as One. This was near the end of our course of sessions and, appropriately it was the autumn.

"I find myself in a dark cave," he said. "It is very frightening, because here are three shapes in the darkness, which I can only dimly make out as women. When my eyes get adjusted to the darkness I will try to describe them.

"The first one is very young and she is veiled. I can't see any glimpse of her face. The second one is completely wrapped in a black shawl. The third is just a black huddle on the floor of the cave. Ah, now I can see her!" I felt Owen's recoil. "She has the head of a black panther!"

After this not very heartening apparition of the Triple Hecate, Past, Present and Future, Owen became aware of the Sage behind him. One of the women gave the Sage his own Moon Brooch. I wondered if Owen would stop here, and return from trance. But in this event I felt that in future he would turn more and more to some spiritual male Master, and have a very natural prejudice against The Fates, and possibly women generally. He would not have passed his feminine initiation, the transmutation of the emotions.

However, the Sage beckoned Owen to follow him, and they left the cave. I was interested to note that the Three Women came along too, and so were not left plotting in the cave, and so in Owen's subconscious up they all went into a high mountain, the Sage, the Women and Owen. And they stood, all five of them, waiting for the rising of the sun.

Slowly the darkness of night gave way to the first rays of the rose and orange dawn. And as the sun began to rise over the mountain, a golden disc appeared in the sky, and floated down towards them. Owen said that a long-haired angel was within this fiery globe. And now a strange thing happened. The three women approached the golden disc as if to ascend into the sky. But first they turned round, and unveiled.

"The first young one," said Owen, "is unveiling her face. And I know her. She is the lady of the well, who gave me a drink from her water-jar. And now the old crone is becoming young. She has thrown off her black shawl. She is the redhaired lady with pearls in her hair, who has the two candlesticks and the golden cup with rubies. And the third one, the woman with the panther's head, she too is changing . . . Now she is a tall and stately Queen with long black hair. They are going upwards, they enter the golden globe, and it rises into the dawn sun-light.

I am left standing with the Sage. And I hold my staff.

I have the right to do so."

So Owen himself achieved the realization that was put into words at the end of his first session in an Arab village:

"Night and Day are one.

"Sun and Moon are one.

"All things are One."

His next stage might unfold in good time. But not with me. Few people can attain beyond the sphere of the psychic; nor should they attempt to do so until they have realized consciousness beyond duality. No high-sounding occult school degrees give true degree. This is only gained through actual development; a natural growth from seed to flower. Real growth is true to nature.

Nonetheless, often unexpectedly, we find ourselves on the threshold of a further expansion of consciousness. We hold the dark key of the sphere of Psyche. We control the waves of the feelings. So may we find ourselves before a doorway with the sigil of the sun. And if the door is ajar, we may enter.

# PART TWO

# THE TEMPLE OF THE SUN

*'The feeling of sun and sea*

# CHAPTER 7

# THE AWAKENING OF
# SOLAR FIRE

MY friends Jean, Lewis and myself were seated in a circle in their home for a spiritualist seance. At least that was what it was intended to be. This was my first time in a circle. We were assembled that evening in their pleasant Georgian room, and a fire burnt cheerfully in the grate. Curtains at both ends of the room were drawn, and only a blue light shone dimly to illustrate Lewis's writing materials. Red light was for physical mediumship, blue for clairvoyance. Jean was not a physical medium nor did she go into deep trance. She received mental impressions.

To begin with, we followed my friends' usual practice of saying together the Lord's prayer as we held hands. Then Lewis described a succession of colours we had to visualize for protection and for harmony. I was thoroughly enjoying myself. I had not up to that time even practised solitary meditation, nor had sat in a meditation group. As for seances, the only one I had even come near was before the war, when the W. B. Yeats and the Lennox Robinsons were going to have one, after my parents and I had left the Yeats' house after tea. And in those far-off days I, an Anglican, had regarded Spiritualism with distrust as 'unhealthy.'

But now I felt very differently.

I remember how cosy it was, that evening, sitting in the firelight, the mundane world shut out, and the unknown about to unfold itself. For I was expecting a possible approach from some relative who had passed on: maybe a cheering message; some little piece of evidence of survival.

Lewis was a careful and thorough director of the circle; putting particular stress on looking after the Sensitive. First, he had the custom of waiting for 'the Gate-keeper', as reported by Jean. After this could come Jean's report of the presence of their Guide and circle of helpers. Only then might some spirit friend contact Jean, and give a message. Of course, as they explained to me, spiritualists never 'called up' spirits. The spirits came if they chose. Jean was at the receiving end. That was all. If nothing were to happen, we would use any power left over in sending healing to those in need, the usual custom in psychic circles.

But something did happen. And it was quite unexpected.

Now Jean announced, not a Gate-keeper or her Guide, but the presence of one who was a Goddess, giving the name of Dana. And as she said this, there came upon the top of my head what seemed like a powerful electric shock. It flowed through my head, and felt like a silvery shower through my body. I felt that to fight it would be worse than useless. Indeed, I liked it. With this came a change in consciousness. I can only try to convey this by saying it was like the impact of hearing a very high note of music, far beyond the span of human voice. It brought wonder and delight. Yet it was so powerful that I feared that if it increased my very flesh might disintegrate. I felt that safety lay in allowing the power to flow freely right through my whole body like a water-fall. It seemed to move in channels in my head, on my brow, at the back of my head and neck. It did not stimulate the fire of the heart, but brought a feeling of purity and happiness.

Meanwhile I listened to the short verbal message that Jean was bringing through. Dana spoke of our valley and of the need for cleansing water. At the time I thought this must refer to an improved water supply, which our village then surely needed. But now I can understand the symbolism, the clearing of the veil that divides one sphere from another. In the Irish is an innate affinity with the spiritual sphere, as yet virtually untapped.

Jean gave a description of Dana, whom she described as having a beautiful and serene face, and long golden hair. She wore white. Now I was able to say that I could recognise this Goddess. By Goddess I meant a being far more advanced spiritually than our race of humans.

Some years before, I had been much upset by a reported cruelty to a cat, and had gone to bed in a turmoil of upset emotions.

Then I had a wonderful experience. I slipped, as it were, right down through the very depths of sleep into another deeper level of consciousness. I saw a most beautiful tall Goddess. Her face was a long oval, with arched eyes of a deep blue colour. Her nose was straight and clear-cut, her mouth small and scarlet. She looked Danish; like a medieval Madonna, or a Pre-Raphaelite Queen. Her hair was golden, and I could see each separate hair had its individual waves. Her long cloak was of a glorious turquoise blue that had the feeling of sun and sea. The edges of this robe, fastened at the throat, were richly embroidered with gold thread that formed an elaborate pattern with her long hair that fell below her waist. I have read of a similar visitation since, described by Fiona MacLeod in his 'Winged Destiny'. He called her the Lady Brigid, the early Irish Goddess, later associated with St. Bridget of the yellow hair.

However, what distinguished this vision from a psychic manifestation was the change in consciousness in myself. For one can see a psychic vision, and yet not alter in any way in one's being. As I saw 'The Gold Lady' I experienced a feeling of the most heavenly happiness. This intense happiness was unlike anything I had ever experienced, nor ever have since. It was not earthly. And now I felt this Lady had come again.

As her mental contact with Dana faded, Jean said that she felt so strong an influx of power in her head that it hurt. I then said I was also feeling this very strongly. We wondered what to do. We decided to hold each others' hands and somehow get the power to channel through, expecting it to disperse. It finally faded, at least to some degree.

Curiously enough, Lewis felt nothing. In fact at the time he was perturbed by this unorthodox change in established procedure. He accepted the uninvited guest as 'a Goddess,' but said why had she not used the offices of Gate-Keeper and Guide? I felt apologetic. And next time she came, not only did Dana make use of the services of Gate-Keeper and Guide, but managed to soften the power she brought with her.

As for myself, after that first evening the power still glowed like a soft light on top of my head and lasted until the next day, especially when I played the piano. I found that "it" was susceptible to mood and thought. So I tried being particularly nice to everybody that day, and avoided arguments or even abrupt words! For I knew that at the hint of any unkindness the Light would go.

And this influence of thought and power has importance on the actual physical level. It was only recently, when reading of the Uri Geller experiments with fork bending, that I remembered a strange happening in a Dublin society many years before. I had gone to hear a lecture on healing. At that time I had read nothing of 'Kundalini' force, or of Solar Fire. I was standing talking to the lecturer after the meeting. That was all I can remember myself of the incident. But a week or so later, a member of that audience contacted me, and told me of a puzzling happening. She said that she had been standing near the healer and myself after the lecture, and was aware of her need for healing. Suddenly, from the direction of the healer and myself, came a shot of electric power. She did not mention this to us. However, when she got back to her flat, she took out her latch-key, which was in the pocket on the side where she had been struck by the 'ray' of power. To her amazement, this steel key was bent double! There was no possibility of getting it in the lock. Yet it had been perfectly straight before the meeting.

She was a determined woman, obviously; one who liked to get to the bottom of things. So off she went to a locksmith, and asked could she have bent the key herself with her fingers, absent-mindedly? He said no, that this was not possible. She told him the story. He could think of no explanation. Next she went to the healer and asked him. He later told me that he had no idea of what had happened, and anyway was not keen on being held responsible for bending keys! Then she searched me out, and found me respectably at the Vegetarian Society. I was taken aback by the lady's story, and denied any knowledge of it. It was only after study and development over some years, that I began to have a glimmer of understanding of what had occurred that evening.

Perhaps the best way of describing this virtually unknown power is a first-hand account of my own acquaintance with it. My brother Alexander first experienced it many years ago when he felt a shock like lightning up his spine. This was accompanied by religious experience.

With me, the development was very gradual, so less terrifying. Years ago I used to attend lectures by an Indian teacher, and it was there I felt a feeling in my heart like a warm orange flower gently burning. It was hard to discover what this was, because it affected my consciousness with a love that was a state of being. I remember trying to control this intensity of devotion by smoking Abdullah cigarettes!

My Heart Centre fluctuated in development through three years. I had read nothing about psychic centres in the body that Indians call 'chakras'. Certain books brought on this feeling. Yogananda's 'Autobiography of a Yogi', and Romain Roland's 'Life of Ramakrishna' affected me very strongly in this way: also the biography of the Monk Tripitaka, by Arthur Waley. The heart centre sensation would last for about a week.

After some years a change came. One evening I went to what I thought was Evensong in an Anglican church in London. I became aware that something was causing a strong silvery tingling in my throat, from the back of my neck. This had a psychic effect of some impact on my soul. I thought it might be healing for a slight cold. Then suddenly I knew what was causing this. I was not at Evensong. This was Benediction. And the Exposed Sacrament was quite definitely radiating a force that was affecting my Throat Centre.

In fact each time a new centre developed in me, it was conveyed to me from a source outside myself. The next time I was aware of this centre was at a healing meeting led by Brother Mandus of the World Healing Crusade. I noticed that these beautiful radiations, as the Holy Spirit, came where they listed, unexpectedly. Also any good channel was used, whether Christian, Hindu, Buddhist or Spiritualist. The power seemed to be a blend of the psychic, because it was affected by thought and feeling. For instance, in my peaceful Dublin flat I kept the silvery psychic lamp in my neck alight for a whole week, because I was in a serene state of mind. Then I decided I could venture forth from my one-woman convent, and have lunch in town. All went well at first. Still my silvery lamp kept alight in the beautiful garden of St. Stephen's Green. But when I met some friends for lunch, I fell. Or rather I allowed myself to be extremely irritated by someone. The light began to flicker out. And, to make matters worse, I began to resent the person for being unnecessarily maddening, and so driving the Holy Spirit away! Not a feather remained. Nor did I get back my serenity for many a long week.

Valentine also experienced this loss. She attained the Heart Centre awakening for three months, during that time being in a state bordering on ecstasy. The experience began in a railway carriage in Norfolk, when she became aware of a Shining Presence that she associated with Christ; or at any rate with someone who had great love. Her own heart awakened. In this state she found that on her return home she loved everyone and every creature, all that existed. And this seemed completely natural. But one day she found herself thinking something unkind and critical about someone. And the state evaporated. She entered into an exaggerated condition of remorse and grief. Then the ecstasis returned. Finally it faded away. How she managed to hold it for so long amazes me. But she lived in the country and met few people, and those were not particularly observant. Otherwise, alas, they might have thought her in danger of a nervous breakdown. For the dividing line is narrow when the etheric part of man begins to manifest. As the rising generation so accurately call such a state, it is 'mind-blowing.'

For myself, I noticed that sound could bring on response in the throat centre. I used to go to an Anglican convent for Compline, and the sound of a gong had this effect. Once a small boy was irritating me very much by rattling empty milk bottles in the garden outside my Dublin flat. I was about to descend in wrath and stop him, when I became aware that the clanging of the bottles had awakened my throat centre! Gesture also could evoke this power. I discovered this shortly before my experience with Jean when Dana came. I was sitting in a restaurant with an ardent vegetarian. She was enthusiastically describing the upward movement of man reaching for fruit on trees. She was, waving her arm and hand. As she did this, I felt a light shower of power fall like a water-fall through my head. This prepared me for my later and more powerful experience. For the sudden onset of power can bring on painful pressure on the top of the head, until the channels are cleared of etheric debris.

So spontaneous development of the psychic centres must lead to a need to control them. I realized that I was moving from the passive world of dreams and trance to the active domain of manipulating power. I was being drawn into the orbit of the Temple of the Sun.

# CHAPTER 8

# CHANNELS OF POWER

IT was Good Friday; and I wanted our house party to be aware of this. We had a cheerful girl cousin staying from Hertfordshire, and were having a good time enjoying the spring weather. But on this day I felt awareness of those who had died through faith in their particular ideals. I am one of those people who insist on sharing their moods with others. So I determined to find a means of doing so! That evening we were sitting round the blaze of an open wood fire in the sitting-room. Alexander was in his big chair; Valentine was in hers. Deirdre, my niece, and the cousin were present. I decided this was a moment to share my own feelings . . . I did not say anything; but left the room and returned with Yogananda's 'Autobiography of a Yogi.'

Somehow I interrupted the general laughter and amusing stories. I began reading aloud the account of Therese Neumann's trance visitations every Good Friday; and commented that doubtless this had repeated itself today. Yogananda described seeing Therese lying in deep trance, pouring with blood from brow, hands and feet. Yogananda put himself into sympathetic psychic rapport, and saw that Therese was witnessing the Passion of Christ. Having gained the attention of my audience, I went on to read that the nail marks that appeared on Therese's hands were square, and Yogananda pointed out that this was like the square nails used in the East . . .

However my reading was abruptly interrupted by Valentine, who suddenly uttered a sharp cry, clapped one hand over the other and shot out of the room.

Afterwards she explained what had happened. She said she could not have explained in front of the cousin. As I described the hand stigmata of Therese, she became aware of a sharp piercing on the palm of her right hand. It hurt. She showed me the marks. Sure enough, in the centre of the palm were four clear cut red pricks, in the shape of a square. These marks lasted for about a fortnight, and then gradually faded out, one by one.

As in the case of the mystery of the bent latch-key, we have a demonstration of the influence of the mind on physical matter. But the mind - this combination of thought, feeling and imagination - does not operate on its own on the body. This is why so many efforts at healing through thought fail. The mind operates through the medium of an etheric power network upon physical matter.

What is this power? One may well ask a scientist to define the nature of electricity. He can tell about the properties of electricity, but not what electricity is. And as 'power' and its area of activity, the ether are as yet unproven, one must fall back upon the experience of oneself and others.

Reichenbach called this Force 'Odic Fluid.' Mesmer, disastrously for his scientific reputation, described it as 'animal magnetism'. Yogis name it Kundalini, Shakti force, a form of prana. I used to call it 'electric-like power' until a doctor told me that it was not electric. Many esotericists use the word 'magnetic', but this apparently is not an acceptable term for scientists. Another doctor told me it was Cosmic Fire - but he was an esotericist. So in our family we used the handy word 'Vril,' from Bulwer Lytton's novel, 'The Coming Race'. His feminine Gy-ei were particularly good at utilizing it.

To the trance psychic, it would appear that our apparently solid earth material is built upon an invisible network, like a spider's web, formed of intersecting channels of force. Our own bodies have a complicated individual pattern of this web, working through certain centres; yet inter-connected with all other beings and things. Indeed one might suppose that the universe is composed of a fantastically complicated spider's web, that yet is formed of one single strand.

Some occult students have seen glimpses of this web. To me it has appeared as either silver or gold. On one occasion I had a vision of silver 'power' flowing through the head of a white-silver Being with whom I associated the name 'Isis'. The power came through the top of the head, in two places, in the form of two great spreading antlers like those of a Royal stag. This may be the silvery power one feels in brow and throat, and at the top of the head.

The gold power I have seen around the head of two figures, who looked like Indian God and Goddess. The figures were made of sunlike gold light. Around each head was a network of golden Power that reminded me of the Phoenix head-dress of China. This form of channelled power was not in two streams, as with the two silver branches. It was in the form of a gold mesh with intersecting lines of power. I have since then seen a similar formation portrayed as headdress on an Indian dancer performing the role of Siva, God of this type of force.

I feel that possibly this gold power is that which one feels in the heart, solar plexus and in the spine. Possibly one sort of power is reflected in the physical form through the sympathetic nervous system; the other through the cerebro-spinal system. For the greater is mirrored forth in the lesser, and a lower level is a microcosm of a permeating higher sphere.

It is interesting to note the social attitude in Homo Sapiens towards the lunar and the solar areas of being. The sphere of the psychic, the passive, is treated as atavistic, domain of women, peasants and gypsies! The field of the magician, however, is respected as belonging to the theurgic power of the Master, who commands the elements.

All our education on this planet is directed to suppressing the old instinctive human psychism, and to developing the rational faculties, controlling practical techniques. I discovered this for myself when I wished to retreat to the psychic passive level, in order later to combine this with the magical sphere.

One can easily test this for oneself. Shut one's eyes. Can one see vividly in pictures? It is pretty certain that if one habitually sees in pictures one is not clever at passing examinations! All our education, with a few exceptions, teach very young children to change from seeing in pictures, eidetic imagery, to thinking in words. The little television set in our brains is short-circuited early on in our scholastic life, and a broadcasting station comes in with brain-washing insistence. One is taught to think in abstract terms, as this is 'higher'. I am reminded of some visitors to the Castle, who walked round our rooms and turned all the objects therein into figures: Pounds and Pence. There are others who turn a book into a 'title', and humans into statistics. Our feelings are classified into psychological terms. One is not shy; one is introverted: not many-sided, but rather schizophrenic. And so forth. This doubtless prepared us to adjust, to structure ourselves into a society which provides us with a flat in a highrise block, and provides us 'assistance' through a numbered form. Human terms are translated into scientific jargon. We are no longer old: we are Senior Citizens. We cannot be poor any more, we are 'underpriviledged.' These are not basically kindly euphemisms. They are de-humanizing abstractions.

Before we computerize ourselves out of existence, we should take a look at what we have lost. For in this area of living we may not take two steps forward without one step backwards. We have lost vision. We cannot see the majority of humanity who are in another sphere - 'dead.' We cannot see Gods or angels. We cannot hear the music of the spheres. And these limitations, ever diminishing our range of consciousness, is also affecting our physical bodies. The spiritually blind soon find they need even stronger spectacles. It is remarkable to note the growing number of people wearing glasses. We cannot hear the music of heaven, so are growing physically deaf. The sound of the cricket and the bat are seldom heard by us. As for our sense of touch - we can feel neither healing being given to us, nor know when healing has left us.

There are those who, faced with the monotony of office and factory life, take refuge in day-dreaming and drugs. They retreat to the psychic realm of the moon, and are classed as maladjusted. Thousands of young people take this course and, rather than live a de-humanized existence in a machine-dominated world ruled by the computer mind - opt out of it all. They try to form an alternative society where art, nature and the psychic once again play a true part.

But to retreat to childhood, however beautiful, is not a sufficient solution. There must be an innate desire to comprehend during the development of Homo Sapiens; and then, not to run away from intellect, but to combine it with the heritage of the man of instinct. Otherwise one can walk around in a dream, unsuccessful in both spheres of day and night.

I feel that the synthesizing agent is 'Vril', Solar Power. And this is as it should be, for the Heart Centre commands the whole body, head to foot. It is through the etheric centres that healing can be channelled through from the psychic sphere to the physical body. And the practical man, the scientist, respects that which definitely affects the physical fields - his own field. The New Elysium needs to manifest on earth, rather than to be banished from earth. For earth is not impure. It is the material used in transmutation, the evolution of mind through form.

When we discover that this power flows through the universal web, we realize that we may transform not only ourselves but those about us, and our surroundings. This transmutation is only effective when voluntarily accepted, and harmonizes with the universal symphony of life. What creature will ultimately refuse love? All nature responds to creative vitality.

Understanding this, we are ready to work actively within the sphere of the sun. We need to learn to bring through that which we have imagined into actual physical existence.

*Enacting a Ritual Drama*

# CHAPTER 9

# CREATIVE HEALING

HEALING means making whole. Yet the word holiness too often conveys the idea of a half person, a floating head, divested by a clerical collar from the rest of the body:- a divided person, the lower part cut off from the higher by a knotted cord at the waist. So humanity sees itself as half angel, half beast, and is anxious to exorcise the beast.

When I began using solar power for contact healing, for a long time I did not attempt to diagnose the cause of a sickness, accepting the medical verdict. I gave healing as best I could through the palms of my hands, using 'Vril' power. I attended healing classes at the Spiritualist Association headquarters. Also, to supplement this, I attended classes on mind healing - a form of New Thought.

The method I began with was the one usually practiced by contact healers. There would be a preliminary prayer, either spoken aloud or in the mind, a request for the aid of healing Helpers from the other world, and I would feel the power come. When it reached my hands, in the form of tingling, I would lay them gently on the patient's head. I had been instructed by a Guide to give healing through the patient's psychic centres. So I would place my stronger hand, the left, near the appropriate centre, the right hand facing the left one. A current of power was then channelled from palm to palm through the patient's body. Spiritual healers claim that their hands are automatically guided by Spirit: that they themselves are used only as channels. In my case I knew that I was operating consciously and had to use my mind as well. For instance through experiment, I found that I could use my gift for palmistry! It seemed more effective in many cases not to touch the diseased area of a patient but rather to run my fingers over the corresponding lines on the patient's palm. I would ask to be told when healing was felt. And sure enough, when I pressed some particular spot on the palm, the patient would report feeling a strong glowing in the sick area.

I noticed that 'Power' was felt by the patient as hot or cold. I found through experiment that by pressing certain areas of the body, for instance, the ankles, I could channel healing through to an affected area. So I guessed that in the mesh of power channels forming the etheric framework of the body, there were certain important pressure points. I had seen these in my vision of the gold mesh about the Indian deities. These points, acting as minor stations of the larger centres of head and spine, themselves controlled particular bodily areas.

Healing then came about through the Healer allowing 'Vril' from the universal web to flow through his own etheric body. To help another he could, either through mental concentration, or bodily contact, re-activate the sluggish, blocked channels of the patient, allowing the life-force to flow through. One could call silver Power the Water of Life that must run pure and free: the golden Power the sacred fire that burns away that which is un-healthy and irrelevant and then brings new vitality.

However, I accepted the need for doctors on the physical level, for I felt that Spiritual Healing was in a sense for the future. It seemed too uncertain to rely on entirely. I know of few mental healers who refrain from going to the dentist . . .

However, though I did not seek to diagnose, leaving that to those with medical degrees, sometimes diagnosis was given to me through my psychic faculty. And this was of a casual sort, pointing out the root cause of the complaint that lay in the soul.

Such an instance came to me when I was giving healing to an Anglican priest: and this case came to typify for me the very root cause of much of our psycho-somatic illnesses. This man typified everything the respectable regard as best in our civilization. He had been an army officer: was intelligent, pleasant, and energetic. He had liked his ministry connected with social work in a poor area, until he had on marriage settled into a middle-class parish. He was the sort of cheerful kindly clergyman you hear on B.B.C. channels, giving forth Christianity to the masses. He had led, I was told, an exemplary life. So why was he suddenly afflicted with an illness that was slowly but inevitably paralyzing him from his feet up, and inevitably led to death?

His fellow priests, he told me, had the habit of sitting round him in a circle wondering what he had done wrong, like Job's comforters. And, as he believed in Positive Thinking and the healthy mind healing the body, he could not make this out himself. It must have been extremely irritating to be an object lesson of sickness, when you yourself could not see any cause. Unlike the Victorians, modern Christians do not seem to regard suffering as being sent to try us. It is more of a challenge to faith.

Anyway, with medical permission, I tried contact healing: but could not channel it through. It was then that I began my first experiments in trance inducing. This worked more easily than getting 'Vril' through. This man understood the technique, and co-operated. At this time I had not imagined that the percipient might leave the Temple I described. This imaginary Temple was circular and white, with a radiating lamp above. This lamp, I said, sent forth rays of healing. It did not occur to me to allow the patient any choice. I went through the usual colour therapy technique: Rose gave forth feelings of love; Blue, of mental peace; together they produced the Violet of Spirituality. The priest could visualize these rays and feel the accompanying ideas, and they helped at the time. But he said the Temple was too like a bandbox! One could not get out.

When on my own, I often asked the mental question: "Why is this man ill?" At last my question was answered! This was the first time that I was given psychic diagnosis. I had a vivid psychic experience one night, more vivid than an ordinary dream. I saw a man's head. He was either Greek or Roman. He was one of the handsomest men I have seen; but I did not like him. His auburn hair was not very long and he had a beautifully kept beard. It was quite different from beards you see now. It had none of the artist or the sailor about it; it looked sophisticated. It was very well groomed. However, I had not much time to admire the gentleman's hair style, for I suddenly became aware of his eyes. They were slanting and grey beneath upturned eyebrows, and were looking straight at me.

And I knew all about him from those eyes! They were the eyes of a pagan soldier, a hero of the past. None could look like that now. They are too suppressed.

However, fortunately for me, the gentleman was inactive for a very simple reason. He had been decapitated.

Next morning I was still much disturbed by this vision, and wondered could this classical looking man be my modern priest? I decided that if this were so, then the soldier was more attractive than the modern vicar. I consulted an occult friend who knew the man. At once she laughed and said:

"Of course: I have seen his face like that. The mask dropped. You watch. Once you see it you will never forget it." I was still doubtful. When I visualized the priest, I could only remember a kindly clergyman with greying hair. However, on my usual day I went off to give healing. And the moment I looked at the priest's eyes I recognised my handsome pagan! For a second his face was transformed. Then he was the nice rather obvious man I had always known.

When one of these revelations come to me in healing, it is followed by an explanation. This came to me later after the priest's death, through a medium who knew nothing about me or this man. This was the story he told me:

"You are interested in a man who has recently died", he said, "despite your healing". This had been brought about by something that happened a long time ago. There was a young priestess working in a Greek temple; and she fell foul of the authorities there because she felt that they were ignoring the intuitional side of their calling. So she was cast out of the temple. This was a terrible thing in those days, for as an excommunicated Priestess none could give her food or shelter.

Finally she was abducted by a Captain of the Guards, a Roman, and stayed with him. The Pharoah of the day heard of this and ordered that the girl should be married to the Captain. Then the married couple were separated. The girl was brought to the Pharoah, who wished to incorporate some Greek practice in the Egyptian rites. This is why from then on there was a Greek influence in the Egyptian Mysteries.

It was only after the sitting that it came to me that the Captain of the past had reincarnated as the present-day priest! But why the paralysis? The doctors said that medically this came from atrophy of the nerves at the neck . . . I had a sudden flash of intuition. The marriage had indeed been short-lived. The Pharoah, expressing his piety in no uncertain manner, had had the Captain's head cut off. It made me feel distinctly peculiar, having seen the head so recently.

Accepting the proposition that everything that exists is connected with everything else; that the greater reflects itself in the lesser: we can understand the law of affinities. Many psycho-therapists notice the correspondence of mental characters with physical ones. One can relate a virtue or a fault with physical health or lack of health. In my own experience working with trance therapy, these correspondences appeared to span many earth existences. This proved itself to me by the fact that percipients in trance, often uninterested in reincarnation, would yet live through episodes of a previous existence that would shed light upon a present problem. Admittedly full knowledge of many lives may only be unveiled by touching the greater sphere of Spirit, which includes all previous incarnations. But it is possible, through the use of psychic faculty, to contact those who do know the Helpers. They can give us needful information from their own wider knowledge.

In my own work I ask that any episode shown to the percipient should be of use. This applies to dreams, psychic experience, and indeed to life itself. First, one learns to master one's dreams. Later, in psychic consciousness, one learns to cope with the experiences of past lives. Only then can one hope to have true free will, the will to choose what one really desires. Up to then, so-called free choice can be a mockery, a limited control, continually eroded by outside influences.

Although control of the psychic sphere can to an extent be obtained without awakening Solar Power, any contact with the more powerful occult forces brought through from the greater level of Causal Mind requires some use of 'Vril'.

After all, what is the point of the patient - the psychic - forever being at the passive, receiving end of Power? Frequently misunderstanding arises because psychic passivity is held to be the role of femininity: the use of occult force, the dominating part of men. As far as my own experience goes, the use of Power in an active or passive sense is an individual attribute, not restricted to one sex.

During my studies of 'Vril' I worked with two other women, Fiona and Angela. I have learnt that three women form a very active combination. At first we specialized. I was the Operator and the Healer: Fiona, the clairvoyant; Angela, the Interpreter. Then we decided to change roles, and so extend our area of usefulness. I increased my clairvoyance and interpretative faculty: the others learnt from me the induction of 'Vril'.

A human being is a focus of both solar and lunar power. As far as I can see clairvoyantly, lunar power works through body and mind: solar through heart and plexus: and by developing the appropriate thought and feeling, all of one's centres become co-ordinated through the spinal channel.

I began to teach those in whom I induced trance to do the same thing for themselves. In any circles that I ran at the Castle I encouraged all-round development. Hence, there was no resentment at one person being the Operator, manipulator of Power, and the others being passive. After all, a human-

being has both right and left arms and legs! We need balanced development.

Nonetheless, I was sure that every single one of us had our own original power structure: that the occult make-up of women was, thank goodness, different from that of men: and that when we tapped Universal Source of power, yet we maintained our own true key-note, our particular wavelength. In harmony with ourselves we could still be in harmony with everything else. In this state we should be perfectly healthy.

Yet we were not. What was short circuiting our vital flow of health from mind to body? This was my next aim - to seek an answer.

# CHAPTER 10

# MIXING THE ELEMENTS

THE most extraordinary case of divided consciousness that I encountered was that concerning Rudolph. He did not come to me for therapy, but rather to investigate reincarnation. But he had been in hospital many times, and our sessions came to include healing. His symptoms included a feeling of strangulation: especially when meeting important clients in his work: and an inability to leave the area in London in which he lived. If he went further afield, he told me, he had a sensation of horrible tension which made him run out of a restaurant or office. This stultifying trouble had continued for ten years, and no medical treatment had done any good.

Then one evening's work gave us a possible cause. That afternoon. before setting off for Rudolph's flat, I listened to the first act of 'Tannhauser' on my transistor. I enjoyed the scenes where the hero disported himself with Venus and her followers in the medieval setting of the Venusberg. In fact I was disappointed at having to miss the next act, which I knew took place in the Hall of the Knights. I had seen the opera as a schoolgirl, and remembered the Ruler of the Kingdom had a niece called Elizabeth, a virtuous female who later became a nun. As a girl I had loved the disgraceful behaviour of Tannhauser . . . when the troubadours had sung respectable songs about love, 'Victorian' in tone, Tannhauser had seized a lute and, having begun quietly, broke into the infamous strains of The Hymn of Venus! The scene was hazy in my mind, though I knew the music well. The whole company of knights drew their swords: and the ladies had fled from the hall, and I knew that the opera concerned itself with Tannhauser's long pilgrimage and penitence. It is important to realise that this opera was in my mind during the afternoon, but not on my hours' journey to Rudolph's flat. Anyway, I had only heard the first act. I had forgotten it by the time I arrived, and did not mention it to him.

We began with my usual prayer to God that we might be given any vision that would be of interest and use. And now came a long and strange story from Rudolph, that gripped my attention so much that I had difficulty in remembering to take notes.

As he lay on his bed, in semi-trance state, still conscious, he described himself as standing in a medieval courtyard. It was not well kept, and had chickens pecking about. He felt his clothes were uncomfortable . . .then he found that he was wearing armour! I gathered that he had been out on some foray. Now Rudolph showed signs of uneasiness. When asked what was troubling him, he said it was the presence of a lady, who was standing in a corner of the courtyard by the castle. This lady wore a high white pointed head-dress and a gown of red and yellow. He said she wanted to marry him.

He longed to escape. There was a grassy bank by the river outside the courtyard, and he avoided the lady and went there. At this point Rudolph was silent for a long time, and I felt that he was unable to enter more deeply into the scene. To involve him further, I suggested that he should look at his own reflection in the water.

"I can't see me:" he said at length. "I am seeing somebody else. It's a boy. Some sort of peasant."

The boy had yellow curly hair, he said, and rosy cheeks. He was averse to saying more about this boy. Instead, he described himself returning to the courtyard, and making his way into the hall.

Now I had the curious feeling that I was somewhere familiar. For Rudolph said that the knights and the ladies were here. Surely I was not being given the second act of Tannhauser, which I had regretted missing on my transistor?

Rudolph did not like the knights nor the ladies. They were, he said, stuck-up. But clearly he wished to be accepted by them. Then he described the throne at the far end of the room. It was an empty throne, and above it was a rather shabby red canopy. At the back was the emblem of a Black Eagle. The castle and courtyard all sounded homely and medieval. Perhaps in those days chickens did peck around among armoured men in courtyards.

Then Rudolph began laughing. He said that the company were making game of a monkey that was playing around in the centre of the room. I was not particularly amused at this: but Rudolph was now totally immersed in his medieval role, and laughed in a jovial way at the little monkey. I supposed they would also have made mock of a dwarf or a hunchback.

Then Rudolph began showing signs of extreme tension. He said he was suffering a terrible feeling of strain that was going to break. I wondered what to do - whether to bring him back from trance, or let him live through the adventure.

Then he cried out loud: "I have done it! They are backing away from me".

Was this the climax? Could he now return? But Rudolph, so far from feeling better at this outburst, seemed to be in still worse mental state. He could not return from trance in this condition. Finally I asked him: "What is happening?"

He said: "The Lady has had her revenge. She informed on us to the King. The soldiers took the boy away in a wooden cage ... They burnt him as a witch."

This seemed horrible enough. But still Rudolph had more to undergo. I waited: then again asked him what was happening. He seemed to be suffering acutely. He replied:

"I hanged myself."

When I brought Rudolph back, we discussed the experience. I told him of the correlation with 'Tannhauser'; but he did not accept this suggestion that he had tapped my subconscious mind. He said that the whole story was symbolic and confirmed entirely his own theory regarding the elements of consciousness. The Lady in red and yellow, he said, with her white pointed head-dress, represented the air-fire elements of mind and will. So also did the court, the throne and the Black Eagle. The monkey was a symbol for the suffering beast that is man. As for water and grass and yellow-haired boy, these all, he said, represented the elements of water and earth. The climax of the story illustrated the total suppression of the emotions by the intellect and will.

But this did not entirely satisfy me. Could there be any reincarnation link? When I returned home, I had another look at the

Tannhauser legend. I made up my own theory. Perhaps there really had been a princely ruler whose emblem was a Black Eagle. He may have had the anything but pleasant niece or daughter, whose jealousy led to her lover's death. What had Tannhauser been doing, anyway?

I remembered that the boy had been burnt for being a witch. The Venusberg, in this case, could have been a pagan site in a cavern, up some rocky mountain in Middle Europe. Tannhauser and others, then, were in a coven that gathered in that remote place. They practised old fertility rites as had their ancestors, and so mingled with the peasantry. It had been the custom, I had read, for men and women to exchange clothes. I could well imagine the fury of the pious Lady on discovering this. Why did she act as she did? Obviously the aim was to kill the boy, not her lover. But the lover committed suicide. In grief, like the heroine in the Wagner opera, she took the veil, and spent the rest of her life praying for her lover's soul.

In this story one doubt remained. I could not quite see this particular 'Tannhauser' hanging himself for the sake of the boy. He had not the depth of feeling. Then I remembered reading that 'the devil' used to hang witches with a rope in their cells, to save his votaries from the stake: but in reality the local squire or some such important person could have been implicated in witchcraft. So what really happened was that the witch who had been imprisoned was strangled by a coven member, before he could implicate his fellows while under torture.

Somehow I didn't particularly like the feel of the Princely Ruler with his black eagle. Perhaps he was high-priest, up there in the Venusberg. To avert scandal, Tannhauser, as well as the boy, had to be sacrificed. And, in my romantic version, Rudolph had been a reincarnation of the unfortunate knight. I wondered would he ever meet the lady who betrayed him, and take an inexplicable dislike to her.

One of the interesting facts that struck me during these sessions, thirteen in all, was the development of 'Vril' in accordance with Rudolph's state of mind. I began each session with contact healing. Rudolph's head and throat centres were totally unawakened. But he responded strongly to healing in his lower centres. Here, I reflected, was the reverse of the Anglican Priest. The Priest's head had been psychically developed: but his body had been slowly atrophying.

This man on the other hand was alive up to his waist but not vital in head and throat. And each man's character and beliefs corresponded to the state of their etheric centres. The priest had died from paralysis. Rudolph, burning with an inner fire, might get another sort of sickness: heart disease - something like that. The Priest had followed the right-hand path of the mind: Rudolph, the left-hand path of the subconscious.

Corresponding with his psychic vision of the Castle of the Knights, Rudolph during our sessions began to awaken in his throat centre. This came about through my giving direct contact power through the throat and to the head. Then, while he was in semi-trance, I asked him to feel this Power flow in a healthy way, according to his needs. On the evening that the Power was raised from the base of his spine to break the barrier at waist and throat, Rudolph had a vision of the sea. He was lying by the shore. He saw a vision of Aphrodite. As this happened, he felt Power like a spray of water loosen tension in his neck. Then the flow entered his head. I noticed that the heart centre was not as yet responding.

I thought that there might be some chord in the 'Vril' octave of the etheric body. One line of power seemed to stem from the base of the spine, work itself to the solar plexus, from there to throat. This chord seemed to me to affect men particularly, giving strength to legs and back and neck. The other chord in the etheric body appeared to run from the sex centre to the heart, and from there to 'the Third Eye'. This chord appeared to be the gentler minor key for woman, giving power to bear children, and brought compassionate feelings, and the soft luminous eye of the dreamer. But both chords finalized themselves in unity at the top of the head. Or, as some say, just above the head, focus of Spirit.

So Rudolph was activated by a masculine chord. He had, anyway, a very strong, almost over-developed solar plexus and neck. His further advancement, then, could be to develop his 'feminine' chord of feeling and vision.

But this further evolution of one's unrealized potential, I guessed, usually came from outside. As I thought about Rudolph, I remembered that his visions used to end with a gold wedding ring. This was his unrealised desire. But where was the lady?

The Lady of his medieval visions I saw in my mind's eye as a nun-like creature: tall with slanting pale grey eyes and long pale lips - an aristocratic German type, like a Cranach painting. In that case she would be the exact opposite of the rubicond portly Rudolph. And how he hated her! Amused, I thought that suggested a possible polarity. When people express a violent hate against someone, it frequently means that they are secretly attracted by 'the enemy', and are bent on suppressing the fact.

For a moment I speculated on the Boy as polarity. No. He was too much like Rudolph. The two of them were like naughty children, refusing to use their brains. Besides, Rudolph rather despised the boy, and would be likely to bully him. He had a hankering to be part of the court and of the Order of Knights.

Anyway, whatever the interpretation of Rudolph's experience, whether psychological, symbolical, or occult, it proved good. When I returned to Ireland, I received a cheerful letter from him, which I still have. He said that since our sessions he never had any symptoms of strangulation. Not only that, he was now able to go where he liked, and was no longer restricted to a small area around his flat. So his pilgrim's staff had flowered. He was ready now to meet the lady if he wished it.

So the uniting of the elements of consciousness within oneself led to uniting with someone outside oneself. This fitted in with my experience as amateur palmist. I had never met anyone who did not, when I read their palms, demand their Beloved! I remember being asked to read the palm of a silvery-haired lady whom I thought well past any such dreams. But she was indignant when I said I could not see a marriage! And if some turn aside from the loves of men, they embrace rather the immortal love of a God. They choose the spiritual rather than the physical form of polarity. For the spiritual far exceeds the physical in beauty. For here all the centres are activated, and link with the divine network itself.

So I hoped that Rudolph might meet his Lady when the time was ripe. Before that time they might well meet, and hate each other.

I came to the conclusion, then, that contact healing and the uniting of the elements of fire and water, heart and head, led to the inter-linking of the separated human consciousness with all other humans, and finally with all nature. Each heart must then be linked with all other hearts, and this was not a sentimental platitude but actuality. And so all minds were linked with all other minds. But one should be protected from too great a flow of feeling and thoughts for others. One was surely guarded by one's individual will and choice. For who would wish to lose his own mind and feelings in an unindividual cosmic soup?

Once, in the wilderness beyond the yew walk, I saw the heart of a tree. I saw it with my eyes open, and watched it for some time. The tree was one of a circle of conifers that formed a natural outside temple. This was the focal tree in the East. Its heart was about four feet from the ground. In colour it was crimson and, curiously enough, 'heart-shaped'. It was surrounded by a ring of gold light like a halo.

I was pleased and honoured at seeing this. It was only later that I realized that I was able to observe this heart, because my own had been in resonance. So it is with us all. What we like intuitively turns out to be true and real. And this encourages us to continue on our quest.

# CHAPTER 11

# THE MAGIC
# OF RITUAL DRAMA

UP to now I had worked with either one person in trance, or with a group practising meditation. The only physical work I had undertaken was that of contact healing, using the force of 'Vril' for cure and to induce trance. Now, however, I became aware of the need for creative beauty that links our earth life with other spheres. Through painting, music and sculpture I realized that a human being linked himself with inspiration from spiritual source.

In the past, inspiration was accepted as being necessary for artistic creativity. The Muses were invoked to inspire their appropriate medium. Later, when people lost their faith in outside inspiration, this degenerated into a mere poetic tradition. But when true communion still obtained between Gods and humans, there was the cult of the God Apollo, and that of the Goddesses.

Minerva bestowed divine inspiration for philosophy, which would then be transmuted into words from the writer's mind. So the artist, as well as the priest, was regarded as a medium. Later, during the humanist revival of the Renaissance, came the cult of the incarnated demi-god called 'The Genius.' The word itself came from the concept of incorporeal beings, the Djinns of Arabia, elemental spirits.

Artists, when held to be divinely inspired by the Gods, had the virtue of humility. Like the present-day mediums, they declared themselves to be channels for the aflatus of Spirits. But those incarnated demi-gods, the Geniuses, knew no such modesty! Their stock-in-trade was their aggressive originality. The cult of the

Genius particularly flourished when I was a young girl. Not in those days did the young hope to be saints, and day-dream of performing miracles, to the amazement and edification of their relatives. Rather did the young hope that they might be a genius like James Joyce or Hemingway. I remember laughing within myself at so many university students confiding in me that 'someone says I am a Genius!' There were so many of them. The only disadvantage to being a genius like Beethoven or Michaelangelo was that one's family and teachers expected some great work to appear! After all, when saints were popular, they were expected to perform miracles.

Hence the prospective genius would retire into his bed-sitting-room, remote from his bourgeois family, later to emerge with a work of art, safely incomprehensible. He was not of today, but of the future, and would only be appreciated then. Meanwhile he could be as weird as he chose! I say 'he' because I did not come across female 'genii'. Glamour was more our aim: we inspired the gen-iuses, who made peculiar paintings of us, or wrote us lengthy involved poems.

Now, studying the occult, I took another look at the question of 'inspiration' and 'geniuses'. What was it all about? I had read of Pyrrhian Fire and Afflatus: of Newton hearing voices: of William Blake conversing with sundry spirits at night. Perhaps he had!

I always like to prove things to myself from actual experience. And in this matter I had the most unexpected instructor. It began with an actual psychic vision. I saw, eyes open and in waking consciousness, the head of a young man lying prone. He had curled hair that had been gilded. His face was Greek in shape, save for slightly high cheek-bones. His eyes were closed. Otherwise lips and chin were so like those of a Greek statue, that I thought for a moment that the face was made of marble. But it was of flesh of a deathly hue: A flesh that had been painted. Not made up with our blended creamy colouring: but actually painted delicately like a picture, with carmine on cheeks and lips. The shoulders were very broad, and draped across with a cream-coloured wool material.

What struck me about the face was its expression. He looked like a very petulant and sulky 'Pop-star'.

Later, cross-reference with an occult friend identified this young man. He was, she said, Antinous, favourite of the Emperor

Hadrian. He had appeared to another of our friends during a Mithraic ritual. Then he had worn his hair long, but still had the same fed-up expression. He was strikingly handsome.

Finally we got through his story, which we found extremely interesting. Not that is, about his earth life, but about his posthumous career as a god! It was in that deified form I had seen him. For after his alleged suicide in the Nile, his corpse had been taken out, embalmed, painted, and his surviving spirit decreed a god of manly sports and exercises, under the aegis of Apollo. He had, he told us, been given work to do, for that was expected of gods, like the hard-worked royal personages of our days. His office or welfare department was his temple, his medium, a priest. How did he appear to us? He tried to come through directly, using my friend as a medium: but then declared that this was not the intention of our group. He found it more difficult to project his appearance and voice to a sensitive, but learnt to do so.

What we gathered was that defunct Pharoahs and other notables who were 'deified' after death acted as spirit guides, healers and helpers. If provided with the necessary power, they could work 'miracles': that is, produce manifestations. Offerings were helpful, in that they provided psychic counterpart, used by the god concerned. This could take the form of 'ectoplasm' or lifetrons — psychic atoms. Prayers, incantations and singing could also give the god or goddess necessary power.

This gave me insight into ritual observances in churches. I had often heard sceptics wonder why God liked so much bad hymn singing! The vibrations of sound, and the effort put into such singing through concentrated thought and feeling could be used for the intention of the group by the deity concerned.

As regards the particular reason for Antinous contacting us, he wished to explain what his present work was. He had incarnated since Roman days, and was now primarily concerned with working for world peace. In fact, in character he reminded me of members of the Society of Friends. He had, we gathered, always liked music, and the simple life of woods and fields. He commented that he liked the simplicity of our way of meditating.

Why, I wanted to know, had he appeared looking so miserable at a revival of a Mithraic rite? He gave the answer that though the true religion of Zoroaster, that of Mithra, was pure and solar, concerning itself with the right use of power, to defend the weak, it had in the latter days of Rome become too much entangled with blood cult. In fact his expression was understandable: as apparently during his initiation he had been deluged with the blood of a bull!

I could imagine how disgusting this would be, as Valentine had endured a similar initiation when a little girl of five. Her father, an M.F.H., had, she said, advanced on her after a kill with the bleeding pad of a fox. While she screamed, he had smeared the bloody torn-off pad down her cheek. She had continued to scream all the way home. Her usually kind nannie would not wash off that blood mark in her bath. It had by tradition to remain until next day. And the memory remained, as it was intended to do. The effect had been the same with Antinous. His subsequent drowning had produced the disagreeable psychological effect I had seen on the face of the newly created god. I understood his partiality for a world freed from violence.

It appeared to me, therefore, that ritual, whether pleasant or unpleasant, affected the subconscious mind of the participant, not only in this life but in the next. When one moves from the passive to the active role in para-psychology, one is changing from trance experience, to the induction of power from one sphere to another. I noticed, when I began making friends with occultists, that they used a different, revealing phraseology as compared with mediums. When faced with a problem, they would say: 'I am going to do something about this!' Having little faith in most people's 'expertise' in magic, I would beg them not to do me any good! I would rather be left alone.

When people have taken a course in magic, they usually want to try out their new skill. They look around for areas where their help is needed. And then they start 'manipulating the web.' And even a beginner can do this, with possibly unpleasant effects on himself and others. A reckless youth in a drunken state in charge of a high-powered motor-car is less of a public menace than some amateur occultist! Such an enthusiast, having read a few books, experimented with drugs, and joined some questionable 'order' then proceeds to use the force of ritual magic. It is not enough that our planet is being threatened by misuse of physical science and that we face extermination through possible nuclear war and industrial pollution. Some ignorant occult practitioners try to affect the etheric web as well; so threatening the patterns of thought and feeling of those around them.

However, the scope of occult misuse is at the moment small. We have lost so much in the non-material field that our quickest way to affect physical matter is still to use physical means. Maybe one can bend a fork if one concentrates enough. But one could better employ the energy in creating a beautiful piece of jewellery. Beauty exerts a more powerful impression on the mind of those who see it than any mere show of 'force'. For humanity responds finally to the great realities of love and beauty and truth. Anything else, however showy, ends by boring us. The first time one is shown a scientific wonder or occult demonstration of power over physical matter, one is impressed. The second or third time, one loses interest. I noticed that the great exploit of man landing on the moon only attracted surface attention. Emotionally we were unmoved. 'Pop' stars who appealed to the feelings still adorned the walls of the young: I never see a 'pin-up' of an astronaut.

In my study of the use of occult force, I realized that we humans are not fundamentally interested in force for force's sake. We have an inner longing for a world of drama and beauty; for wonder and surprise. This may be brought about by first acquiring money and worldly importance: but few regard these as ends in themselves. Examine people's day-dreams: they express the need for affection and beauty. There are few who see divinity expressed in terms of scientific formulae, though such rare people do exist. Most of us, however, are stage-struck. We wish to act in the theatre of life in an emotionally satisfying way; to identify ourselves with what we admire: to receive the plaudits of the multitude.

And the Western school of the Mysteries caters for this. We of the West tend to be actors. We like working and playing with other people. We are gregarious. We like splendour and pageantry and glory. And to get any good out of it, we must be presented with an exciting, moving part to play in the drama of life.

I roughly classify 'the West' in this way, although there are natural quietists in the West, and exhibitionists in the East. As Hari once said: 'The Quakers are the Brahmins of the West.' Maybe. but there are not many Quakers. One realizes, studying our newspapers, novels, films and television, that we feed on sensationalism.

And why not? Admittedly the higher path is to withdraw from 'the dream of life'; to enter a Trappist monastery or enclosed convent, and live a life of prayer. But most of us want to join the processions, the revolutions, the happenings. Whether at funerals or weddings, crowd scenes appeal to us. Need we be ashamed of this? The great Christian Mystery is essentially dramatic. And after all, although in the crowd, we need not shout 'crucify him,' but rather be among those who shouted Hozanna, and strewed palms in the way.

In my work with those in trance, I noticed what exciting adventures people had! I enjoyed them myself. The adventurer would have a release of pent-up emotion in fighting in his joust, in facing a dragon, in rescuing a princess. But nonetheless, the body still remained totally inactive. I found it hard to persuade some such psychic pilgrims to meditate on their own - to do something useful in everyday life. Could there be any half-way zone between trance adventure and daily work? Otherwise I was only giving a substitute for drugs and dreams.

I tried the experience of attending church service with these students. I myself could participate. But they found the part there was too inactive. As one girl said: one knelt, sat, got up, and sang, and that was all. The priest had the more interesting role; but only the priest. The 'audience' as she called it, sat barred off from the chancel, the stage. She was bored and would not go again. I found the same reaction with others. They resented being at the receiving end of a ritual. Nothing was happening. Life outside at least promised them activity. They could not be passive.

It came to me that a new age was bringing about a move from passive to active role among our planet's millions. Up to now, in church, one knelt meekly on one's knees facing the place of transcendental Deity. Only a select and trained band of priests or Brahmins could be channels for Deity and stand in the Holy Place. But now the neophyte, whether man or woman, expected to be a priest: to stand in the appropriate position, and act as channel for the Deific Presence.

We were moving, as had been prophecied, into the era of God the Holy Spirit: of Pantheism. Innate Divinity could be realised by those willing to express this divine power, that is latent within all existences.

The interlinking area between the spheres of Divinity and the earth sphere, was that of the Temple of Ritual. For the law of Octaves of sound prevailed throughout the universe in the law of correspondences. Strike a note on one level, and you produce a corresponding response in the sphere you wish to contact. Make a symbolic gesture on this plane with deliberate intention, and you affect the area on which you are concentrating.

Each of the five senses, then, had an affinity with supernatural senses. And one could only understand sacred scriptures, the Bible, Bhagavadgita, the Sutras, if one read them with heightened faculties, understanding this law of affinities. So 'sight'. 'hearing', 'touch', and so-forth each had an inner meaning to the initiate - that is, one who had been awakening to this level of awareness.

So one could recognise the mysteries performed in daily life: the ancient Greek dramas producing their archetypal effect through living men and women. Such playwrights as Ibsen, Strindberg and Yeats were consciously aware of this, and drew it to the attention of the audience. Through art, a human-being could identify with Ulysses, Oedipus, Elektra, or indeed the Chorus.

The only difference then, between great drama presented to an audience, and the Mysteries, was that the Mysteries were not for an audience, but brought each performer into meaningful participation with the enacted drama. The neophyte identified with the questing Psyche in her search for Eros; with Orpheus seeking Eurydice in the netherworld. According to his own development, he underwent each deepening layer of consciousness: Stage One, Stage Two, Stage Three. Each stage brought its peculiar ordeal. And, according to his capacity, he succeeded or failed. Success meant permission to advance further. Failure was no disgrace. It merely meant that the candidate was not yet ready to undergo further trials, at any rate during that life-time. He would try again and one life-time he would succeed!

And yet even these Mysteries were not fully realized, lacking embodiment on earth. The greatest, because the most inclusive, of these divine dramas had to happen in every-day life: have a human face; a physical environment. I realized that, however well one might cope with lunar initiation through trance experience, it really was easier than having to face actual physical happenings. It was, for many of us, easier to be 'dead', in the psychic sphere, than to live well on earth. Thus Solar Initiation, inspired living, was the next stage to be faced. And, looking around at the world, one could see that we were nowhere near achieving it. Some of us had good ideals, fine dreams. But could we bring them through successfully into earthly actuality? That was what we had to learn: to achieve the union of heaven and earth.

# CHAPTER 12

# INITIATION OF THE SUN

BEFORE the Psyche may arise beyond duality, she must needs unite with her counterpart called Eros. But the divine union of opposites may only be accomplished by self-giving. And this giving of the self may seem to be a voluntarily dying, to those who identify with body and soul qualities. Death is only an ending to those who call the body 'myself'. So is poor self, dead as it lies in its coffin, a decaying piece of disintegrating matter. But to those who have passed through the Temple of the Moon and know the Psyche, there is no bodily death. They have parted the veil. The difference between the Gods and human beings is that human beings believe that they die. The Gods know that they are immortal.

But there is another sort of dying: the second death. Is it possible to be in love with one's own soul, to be infatuated with one's beauty? This infatuation may be the great dividing barrier that separates human consciousness from the Spiritual Sun. The Psyche is freed from identification with the transient five senses. Then, in love with her own beauty, she gazes deep into the pool of her reflected image, and so falls into a trance of self-love. She may only be awakened by her lover, that spirit of divine fire, Eros.

Facing this second initiation of Light, once again there is the fear of death, of self loss. Here is the error of the soul, which clings to its limited existence from incarnation to incarnation. It is at this level that repetition becomes mechanical: that great art degenerates into platitudes: the saintly consciousness diminishes into that of the Pharisee. For if not replenished by the Spirit, the soul like the body disintegrates. In seeking to prolong her enclosed existence in the realms of the psychic, she only has continuity, not immortality.

We have this ordeal of the soul described in Lytton's 'Zanoni,' where one Adept clings to a limited existence for centuries: the other Adept, Zanoni, gives up time for Eternity. For Eternity has nothing to do with the cycle of time. It is all time, is ever present, and knows no past nor future. It is Now.

Hence if the soul has the courage to take the plunge of losing its limitations, it finds not a loss of consciousness; but Cosmic Consciousness. However, this plunge of self-giving must be an act of faith; for who can know that which has only been described by others? The sacrifice of self-identification seems to imply the loss of personal consciousness. Such a surrender will not come from spiritual ambition: from desire for adepthood. It can only come from the love that transcends all thought of 'me' and 'mine' and spills itself out to the Other, which then becomes 'the Self'.

A session with Roderick well illustrated for me this whole enormous problem of self-giving, not of the body, but of the soul.

At the beginning of our sessions, Roderick saw the appropriate symbols of the psychic level: the sarcophagus, the cave, the well. Now, nearing the completion of our work together, he came across the White Tower. This was symbol for the aspiring element of air and fire, that pointed skywards away from the lunar world to the domain of the sun itself.

Roderick reported, as he lay in trance, that he was reaching this Tower not as a little boy or as a youth, but as a Knight. I knew then that our sessions were drawing to an end. His aim had been to identify with Sir Percival, and attain the vision of the Goddess of the Moon. This, he hoped would lead to a union with his ideal Princess.

As in his trance he gazed upwards at the Tower, he said he caught a glimpse of woman's golden hair. He thought that this must be Eloise, the Princess of his dreams. This Eloise had appeared occasionally in his visions in various guises. She bore no resemblance to any girl he had met in this life. In his joust scene in the fifteenth century, she had shown herself as a jolly girl like a milkmaid, with golden curls. During another session, in a seventeenth-century drama, she had appeared as a twelve-year old Puritan girl.

It had always been Roderick's avowed end to declare his love to his Princess in one of his visions. Then he hoped to find her in everyday life and marry her. So I was puzzled now, because he seemed to hesitate, to avoid approaching the visionary White Tower. I suggested that he should enter it. But Roderick was never very easy to deal with - in my way. He replied evasively that he was not worthy of Eloise; and preferred to stay on the ground. The Tower was speaking to him, he said, of the glory of endeavour and of honour. But still he would not go near it; and I felt that we would stay like this until supper time, unless I prodded him to do something.

I came out with every cliche I could think of, including the one about faint heart never winning fair lady. I was reminded of our adventure with the dragon. Roderick had refused to look at the dragon, or to fly over it; he had crawled under. But now he had to go up a Tower - or come back. There was no alternative. He said he had no head for heights. Yet he did not want to give up and return from trance.

He knew that this was his great moment. He stood contemplating the situation. I tried my old dream changing method. "Try and imagine you are inside the Tower," I suggested.

After a pause, Roderick announced that he was climbing up the Tower from the outside. He would not go in. It struck me that he was viewing Eloise with not much more enthusiasm than he had viewed the dragon. Yet, as he slowly climbed, he said that she was his Heart's Desire. He was a tall fine looking man, and I could picture him spread-eagled outside the tower, tortuously making his way up from loop-hole to loop-hole. Finally, I was relieved to hear that he had reached the top window, and was hanging there with his fingers on the window-sill. He peered in. Eloise was there. She had her back turned to him, he said, and was standing away from the window.

"Good," I said. "You are doing well! You have climbed up the Tower, and the Princess awaits you. Enter the room!"

There was a long silence this time. Then Roderick reported: "I've got one leg over the window-sill!"

"Well, get the other one over," I said, trying not to sound irritable.

Then Roderick made a remark that has always stuck in my memory. "I have," he said, "a sort of loyalty to my own half-self. She is my other half. But I feel that it is not for me on this occasion to go in. I think perhaps I shall go down."

This was too much. We had reached the twenty-sixth session. Was all our work for nothing?

"What is Eloise doing?" I asked, hoping she would help him.

"She has turned round," said Roderick, forgetting himself for a moment. "She is looking at me." Then, in a voice of triumph: "I have climbed into the room!"

But still he felt unable to make any approach, and said he was unworthy. I felt that he was overplaying his humility.

"This," I said "is your declared aim, to unite with the Princess! Cannot you speak to her, hold her hand?"

"'No," said Roderick. "She is too beautiful - too perfect. It is not for me at this present moment. I shall come back at a later date."

Of course I could have brought him back from trance then. Indeed, if I were to follow to the letter my own policy of letting people choose what they wanted to do, I would suggest the return. Yet I knew within myself that this would have been to fail his true need. He had asked me to help him, and help him I would! Besides, there was Eloise to consider. What if she were not a mere figment of his imagination, but his true twin soul waiting him somewhere on earth?

I wondered what to suggest. I knew that Roderick would not speak nor touch her hand. Then I remembered that enchantment was said to emanate from a woman's eyes. Yet he would see no danger in that . . . I remembered our friend the dragon.

"Look at her in the eyes!" I said.

Now came the climax. I could tell that Roderick had entered into a state of blissful consciousness.

"I do so!" He said. "I wish I could convey the rapture I feel! Her hair is golden and her eyes are deep blue! She is all that I have hoped for. But strange - her hair changes to red; her eyes have become green . . . Now she has raven hair and black eyes. She is all woman: she is a Goddess!"

I was reminded at this point of the speech to Helen of Troy by Faustus in Marlowe's play. But in the case of Faustus an intention had been expressed to destroy another Troy! Roderick had desire for good. So in his case nothing but beauty and peace would come from his unifying experience. He left Eloise, and came down from the Tower, but this time by a winding stairway within it.

I said: "Now you are a Prince, a Knight - and a man. The vision is ended. Let the power manifest now through you on earth."

But it is a great deal more difficult to manifest good on earth than in the higher psychic sphere. For one thing, the ideal Beloved may respond to telepathic communion: may project easily into one's dreams. In the higher psychic sphere one is at one's most attractive: kind, loving and beautiful. When one has learnt to control emotion, one is not retarded by bodily discomfort — nor even by lack of money! So when Roderick finally left us, I wondered what would befall him in the mundane sphere of daily living.

A year or so later we met in London, and I asked how he had fared. In many ways he had done extremely well. He had published a successful book on his philosophical theories; on the importance of uniting the elements of Fire and Water, Positive and Negative, within oneself. But, I asked, what of Eloise ?

Of her there had been no glimpse. And I could imagine Roderick sitting in a cafe, and for a moment recognising Eloise in the form of a waitress - until she turned round and he faced a stranger. In the street outside, in the din of modern London, might be glimpsed a gleam of golden hair from the top of a bus: the sight of a woman in the distance down a long street. But never Eloise.

What then was the meaning of this pursuit of the ideal? Was Roderick to learn the truth that Eloise was in every woman; and so find ultimate beautitude in a diffused love of all beings? The answer was, I felt, different for each individual. For Roderick, I felt that through this one woman known through many lives he would find salvation. Then, through her, he would love all others. For another sort of man, the Priest, the love of God could come through loving all beings, and then finally manifest through the One. There is the sort of woman who recognises the one in the many: another discovers the many in one man.

Either through devotion to one person, or philanthrophy for the many, Solar Initiation achieves union of the opposites, self and not-self.

To attain the Universal, the stars, one must first transcend duality. It is said that the Master throws no shadow. To clarify this, I once invented a tale of Three Planets. On one planet the people lived beneath a perpetual cloud obscuring their two suns. These two suns of their system shed a diffused light that never faded. These people knew of neither day nor night; bright sunlight or shadows. They lived a respectable if dull routine of existence, feeling neither heat nor cold, and never running to extremes in thought or feeling.

There was a pioneer among these people who managed somehow to gather a group of friends to build a space-ship. Off they went, and reached a planet with entirely different conditions. The people here had one sun only, so at night they were plunged into darkness. Nor had they many clouds; so for the first time our pioneer and his friends saw shadows during the daylight. They observed that the natives of the planet had the peculiar habit of drawing outlines round shadows, whether very long or very short, and then worshipping them as gods and demons!

The natives' philosophy seemed very strange to our pioneer from the grey planet. These inhabitants of the world of light and darkness explained that all life consisted of a battle of opposing forces; one of the light, the other of darkness. To make matters worse, if more exciting, the shadows joined in! The fat little shadows of mid-day were benign and jolly, and helped them. But the long thin shadows of evening were malign and presaged darkness and evil.

Convinced that he had entered a world of madness, our pioneer decided to leave for a visit to a third planet. But his friends would not accompany him. For this third planet shone so brightly, that they took it for a sun. They did not wish to be burnt. So they went home to their own sensible planet, and left the pioneer to his eccentricity.

For his second trip, our friend entered into deep trance, and in this way safely journeyed to the Third Planet. And it was indeed too hot and too bright for a physical body. The inhabitants of the place of light and shade declared our psychic traveller was dead, and burnt his body, their usual funerary custom.

He however ascended in spirit to the Third Planet and found there a world of colour and beauty and people who were self-luminous.

"Ah," he thought to himself: now I know the meaning of the words an old sage at home once repeated to me: "The Master casts no shadow." And he looked down at the bright grass and flowers at his feet. And he also cast no shadow.

So it is only by analogy that one may imagine the domain of the Inner Sun. We are given words such as 'building the solar body.' But I feel that the solar body is there for all of us: we have rather to strengthen the rainbow bridge that joins our souls to our Spirit.

How may we do this?

Strangely enough, in this most active area of the Inner Sun, we must at last surrender activity. In order to transcend limitation, we must give up the barriers we ourselves have built in order to protect our own developing originality.

For the surrender to the Light prematurely is to suffer the fate of Semele, and be burnt by too great a glory. One needs, as the earth does, one's protective veil of blue atmosphere, one's shell of personality.

One is encouraged in approaching the Initiation of the Sun, by seeing the bright form of one who has attained the Light. Once I was awakened in the morning by just a vision. Eyes open, heart full of wonder, I saw standing at the foot of my bed a figure made of golden light. He was self-luminous and shone like the sun. And the glory came from love.

Others have had a like experience. And this Solar body also belongs to ourselves our true greater selves, if we will only allow ourselves to be conscious of it.

Yet this consciousness comes from self-forgetting.

The constrictions of self fall away and, like the butterfly we immerge from the chrysalis of what was once our whole world. We are like new-born babies when we first awaken into Cosmic Consciousness. We lose nothing; rather we gain the harvest of many lives. We touch on the experiences of our own spiritual group.

We have the Universe before us - Temple of the Stars.

# PART THREE

# TEMPLE OF THE STARS

# CHAPTER 13

# STONES AND STARS

IN our small Temple of Isis my two small nieces, aged fourteen and ten, were waiting to dance. Alexander began the enacted scene by playing Schumann on the small Dutch organ. Bernard waited to play the dulcimer that he had made himself. At each stage of the story a different instrument was to take over. Owen had his flute to play at the climax. I was telling the story for the girls to act. The younger dark girl, Rosalind, began dancing in the first scene. She was playing the part of a fairy, a few inches high, an elemental spirit in charge of a very tiny patch of grasses, daisies, buttercups and clover. At first she enjoyed herself. Then, I explained in my narration, she got bored. In her discontent she showed in mime that she wanted to do something a great deal more interesting than looking after a patch of earth with its plants.

Now the organ gave way to the dulcimer. The older fair girl, Helena, appeared on the platform by the statue of Isis carved by their brother Finn. Her style of dancing was different from that of Rosalind. Rosalind danced thoughtfully, working out each movement with her mind and executing it with precision. She seemed to know intuitively movements that looked like those of Egyptian ritual. Helena, on the other hand, danced with the style of a classical Greek dancer. Her movements were free, yet balanced, like those depicted in a Tanagra vase. Both had learnt European Ballet, but recently had been studying the depicted movements of Egyptian, Classical and Oriental styles. We were all of us experimenting. Bernard composed his own music, Indian style. Owen's flute-playing was Spanish sounding, also composed by himself.

The part Helena had to play was that of a Goddess appearing to the fairy that belonged to the same evolving devic kingdom as herself. She played the role with elegant humour, one of those devis born rather than made! She had no self-consciousness at standing with her back to the altar, a living embodiment of the statue.

She offered to show the little girl a greater sphere of activity. So off the two of them went - to the world of animals and men. This sphere was represented in the temple by two small side chapels, one containing pictures of various creatures, including Durer's hare and a Chelsea china lamb: the other containing small images of Buddha and a wooden Venus carved by Finn.

However, though first attracted by the idea of guiding animals and humanity on their evolutionary path, the fairy soon became bored by her role of Guardian Angel. She aspired to the stars.

This was time for Owen's flute playing to take over. The Devi indicated that to accomplish this, the fairy had to go back to her patch of earth. There, amidst the wild flowers and grasses, she was to make a little circle of small white stones. This seemed easy enough. To the high sound of the flute, Rosalind made movements of creating a stone circle. She was then told to stand in the middle of it - shut her eyes, and turn three times round. She did so.

Now the Devi took her by the hand and led her up the three steps to the platform in which stood the altar. She then was told to open her eyes.

I now explained that the circle had become a great spiral of stars: the flowers shone as star dust; and the patch of earth had been transformed into the great void of space. And through the darkness came the unearthly song of the great Gods and Goddesses, the Star Angels.

But this was too much for the little fairy. Overcome by this vastness, she begged, hands clasped, to be allowed to go home to her patch of earth. This the Devi permitted, with a downward movement of her hand . . . Now the sound of the flute gave place to the gentler dulcimer. Helena guided Rosalind down the three steps. As the fairy reached the expanse of flowery carpet, the dulcimer was lost in the familiar deeper sound of the organ. The little fairy found herself once more in the centre of her circle of little white stones. Hastily, she scattered them. She was glad to return to her task of looking after her few plants and little bit of earth.

Usually, when we performed this drama, I let it end there. But later I added one final piece. Helena, as she bade farewell before she returned up the three steps, explained that if ever the fairy wanted another trip to the stars, she had only to make a circle of white stones, stand in the middle, shut her eyes and turn round three times.

For those who have had mystical experience, however overpowering this may have been at the time, will one day, some time, wish to touch a greater level of consciousness again. And why not? It is our goal.

In our Temple my aim in producing these mystery dramas was to create rituals that taught the laws of expanding consciousness. These dramas were not ritual magic in the practical sense: they were not intended to produce effects on the physical environment. Rather were they to affect the minds and feelings of those taking part, in group participation. For what is life as we know it but a group dreaming? Our waking lives have all the qualities of a dream. Dreams are fleeting and disappear with the coming of day. But our waking activities end when we fall asleep. And this waking fantasy of day-time has the effect of involving us totally in the story we call 'life'. Yet when we sleep this 'total' identification is completely forgotten! How transient then is our waking existence! Also, when we learn the art, we can change the pattern of our physical lives as we have learnt to re-create our dreams.

But there is one snag here. We can only change our nightmares to beautiful dreams through the aid of greater consciousness, the all-embracing awareness of the day.

From the vantage point of an active physical brain and the use of will, we can manipulate our dreams and trances. But what greater mind can possibly organize this dream of physical existence, and mould it nearer to our heart's desire? Must we be forever like leaves in the wind, pushed about by circumstances, passive in our weakness?

It is only by awakening into a more universal consciousness that we can truly create our earth lives into meaningful pattern, part of a greater design. Otherwise, blind and deaf, though we think we see and hear, we make false moves and blur our own true ends. And how indeed can we even see that there is a grand design and any relevant part for ourselves within it, unless we can transcend identifications with the passing moment?

Understanding the relationship of past, present and future, we may develop the ability of seeing causes and their effects, forming one related pattern worked through the web of time.

Symbols are the language that help the finite human consciousness to have glimpses of a greater reality. For everything on a lower level is a symbol for some higher reality. So grasses, trees and rivers, and everything that exists on this level, form living symbols of their own transcendent reality in a higher sphere. One's personality is a shorthand of one's true self; sometimes a poor translation. We are like actors wearing a mask that typifies what we wish to be in this life's projected drama.

So in order to go higher, we first have to sink lower. Or, if you like, we have to limit our consciousness still further in order to expand into cosmic awareness. Because if we can through Myth, Ritual or Mystery identify with the play of life itself, we can then see for ourselves that this life also is an illustration of a transcendent reality.

So with organ, dulcimer and flute, with meaningful symbols, with incense and candles, we make a temple that makes sense of the jumbled, apparently meaningless environment in which we have our physical being. Here in the temple, at any rate, is order, and no blind chance. There are no accidents, no irrelevancies in church or temple. The sanctified circle typifies a chosen environment. Bread and wine, paintings, stained-glass, colours for altar frontals, images, are put in a temple with specific intention. The intention is to express a chosen spiritual reality. So a cup represents the Grael; living water: a sword, the element of spiritual fire; a wand; the creative mind. Two stones, one rough and one smooth, are symbolic of earth. Pestle and mortar, hammer and knife, are no mere tools, but have a specialised meaning.

Each note of music used in a Ritual draws down its great meaning, and works upon the being of those taking part in a Mystery. Every word has its archetypal response from higher spheres: so in a temple are no meaningless words. For words are translations of the speech of angels. Not only this. Tablets marked with sigils are a means of communication with beings of brighter worlds: and every dance movement and gesture produce their appropriate effect in the world of causes. For the world of causes produces effects, and so responds to its own echo.

In the intensely meaningful world of the Temple or Church, half-way between physical and spiritual reality, the aspirant learns to recognise affinities and correspondences through the language of symbols. First through dreams, and then through enacted mystery dramas, the neophyte finds his own consciousness beginning to respond. And in this way he learns safely to expand into greater levels of awareness, without becoming unbalanced. Every movement in a Ritual itself brings about balance: and the flow of 'Vril' is channelled through in its appropriate traditional way, without destroying the practitioner's mind.

And this is why it can be very dangerous to use hallucinogenic drugs. Admittedly the use of these can induce mystical experience without work and discipline. But those who, as it were, climb over God's fence into the hidden garden, and steal the apples from the forbidden Tree, may suffer terrible retribution. True, they may and often do, have the vision of Deity and the knowledge of the existence of Cosmic Consciousness. The unfortunate Semele unwisely demanded to see Zeus not as man, but as God; and so was burnt. So may the unwary aspirant who takes drugs destroy his etheric double.

To put too great a charge of electricity through wires means a fuse. A fuse may be repaired. But how does one repair the damaged etheric body when it has been struck by the lightning of Zeus? The Gods do not deny humans the golden apples of the sun through jealousy or selfishness. Only when the aspirant has a psychic and physical makeup ready, can he safely be initiated into wider consciousness. For instance, a telepathic dog, suddenly at the receiving end of the mind of a human Professor, would undoubtedly go mad!

We must then approach the Temple of the Zodiac with caution. It is not enough to have self-sacrificing love. We need that handmaid to wisdom, common-sense. Sure of our emotional control, the moon at our feet protecting our steps, we may attempt at last our ascent to the stars. And to do this, we must learn more about ourselves. Are we ready for cosmic consciousness? Our further step is to find out. We need to face the effects of previous Lives.

# CHAPTER 14

# A DRAMA OF MANY LIVES

ONE morning in London I was not feeling very well; so I lay on my bed, resting. I was not asleep. Suddenly I was transported to another place in another century. Yet I retained enough of my modern consciousness to record what I experienced.

In personality, I was very young and gay. I was moving swiftly through a charming, fairly small room. I knew it to be in a seventeenth-century French chateau, and in time, about 1672. What made the apartment so delightful was that it was panelled in new oak, a pale golden colour. Nowadays one usually only sees old dark oak panels. Moreover, unlike our present custom of leaving oak severely unadorned, the details of the panelling were lightly touched with gilding. This gave a quaint effect wholly pleasing, yet to our modern eyes, inappropriate. Also the room was much more bare than even the most austere of our interiors would allow; for there were no carpets that I could see. The floor was bare wood, beautifully polished. In fact the place looked new, very well kept, shining with cleanliness.

I cheerfully glided through this room into one that directly led from it, about the same size. At the far end of it stood a short youngish man - about thirty, but possibly younger. He was dressed in the costume of the reign of Louis Quatorze, with brown curling wig and neat brown clothes. What struck me was the natural ease with which he wore his clothes, as if they were a part of him: unlike modern actors I had seen in period costume in the Comedie Francaise, and historical plays and films. There was that indefinable reality of clothes worn in their true period.

Anyway, I advanced towards this amiable gentleman, my arms outstretched towards him. My feelings were those of one greeting a dearly loved cousin.

Then, to my unutterable disappointment, I was back in Kensington, lying on my bed! This experience had been as real as my present-day existence. I was convinced of its actuality. It had not been a mere memory of a past reincarnation. It had been a re-living.

This is why the word 'reincarnation' does not entirely satisfy those who have had experience of re-living another life. As the 'Now' of the experience is as real as the 'Now' of the twentieth century, can one say that previous centuries only bring us memories? Indeed, a re-living of a previous moment in the so-called 'past' is more actual in self-consciousness than mere memory of 'yesterday'.

The vital link, then, in reincarnation experiences is the self-conscious awareness of the Now. It is the juxtaposition of 'I' with time passing.

To understand how consciousness works, one needs to study the process called 'reading a book'. When I was a child, I was told by other children how long it took for one to 'get into' a book. Some books took a long time to enter, but were worth it. Victorian books could almost totally involve one, so that, hidden in hay-loft or attic, one lost track of meal-times, of time itself. One was totally identified with 'Jane Eyre' or 'David Copperfield.'

Of course we children knew that such identification was transient: that we had to come back from the delicious trance of daydreaming to everyday existence. And, for book addicts, daily life at school and home was less interesting, however apparently pleasant, than the most harrowing adventures in 'book-land.'

When I was about ten I wrote a book about my own adventures in what I called History Land. My technique was to 'go into' a chosen period of history inside a history book. Each of my chapters recorded various adventures, being killed by druids and priests or being chased by Roundheads! However, when I was about to be decapitated, burnt, or stabbed with a dagger, I would escape from the experience 'through the margin'. As each page of the book had this blank margin, it offered a way out.

And this is exactly what we humans do when we have had

enough of earth existence. Faced with firing-squad, incurable illness, or just an uninteresting old age, we 'go into the margin'. We wake up into the wider consciousness of our own greater selves. We cease to project into the little character we had thought of as 'me'.

At first, studying reincarnation, one is only aware of the experience of one particular person, usually oneself. Other people are mere foils — friends or enemies, or merely there to be audience! The creature called 'me' is real and pleasant. Other people are only seen in relation to 'me', and hence are subjective, and only matter in so far as they relate to the all-important hero or heroine.

Who does not to a certain extent identify with family, nation and one's childhood religion? It is all a part of the area associated with 'me'. Those aliens not associated with 'me' have different coloured skins, strange religions and politics - are different- and so, not being 'good' like oneself and one's friends - are very probably 'evil'!

In trance and psychic experiences of reincarnation, however, there emerges a wider consciousness of one's Group, 'Us'. For instance, in Roderick's trance experiences, for him 'Us' consisted of Eloise, a Hermetic Healer, a Woodsman and a Knight - people he learnt to know and like, though he had not met any of them in this present life. For Owen, the Group consisted of Eloise, a Hermetic Healer, a Woodsman and a smith and a Gypsy. These meant more to him, I think, than anyone he had come across today.

So the criss-cross web of living produces not only awareness of 'me' and 'my' admirers and friends; not only 'them', the enemy, the alien people who don't agree with me or like me, but, gradually, 'Us' my group.

In usual consciousness, we are cut off from other people and the rest of life by lack of true communion of thought and feeling. We have a family, yes - and friends and colleagues - but there is a blank wall when it comes to telepathic rapport. Every man is an island, solitary, until he can touch the universal web of inter-communion. The Communion of Saints is meaningless to us until we experience it in reality.

So man is the most lonely of all creatures. He is the only being that believes in that ultimate solitude, Death. Can anything be more horrible than to imagine losing the ever pleasant friendship with oneself? One's soliloquies, jokes, pleasures? No animal faces such a threat. They do not die as we do. They shed the physical body but otherwise, like Angela's cat, proceed as usual.

So we are more cut off from God than any other being, because we have lost communion with the rest of nature. We talk to each other in words, and through this very cleverness - we lose heart and mind communion. How many times do we, as we argue, lament that we cannot truly communicate what we really mean? In final failure to achieve any true contact - we take to mass violence, killing each other in war.

And even then we sin in ignorance, for hopefully we kill an adversary, thinking to be rid of him, whereas in his soul he stands and watches. So far from seeing the last of somebody we disagree with death only brings the enemy nearer. And he will return to life again, and avenge himself.

I like the story Hari used to tell us of the butcher killing the lamb. Next life the lamb was born as the butcher, the butcher as the lamb. The killing was repeated. This reversal of roles continued for many lives, each taking alternating parts, the butcher and the victim: until one day the lamb sat up, just before the butcher cut his throat, and said: "Hasn't this gone far enough? If you kill me I shall assuredly return and slaughter you in my turn!"

The butcher put away his knife . . .

Would that humanity might do the same.

What can we do to be able to listen to the voice of the lamb, and understand its speech? All we hear now, as we raise the knife, is merely a pathetic bleating - and unpenitent we kill, and eat lamb for lunch.

The answer is simple. We progress in nature's way, despite our petty selves. As we develop, we become more sensitive: and we learn to hear the thoughts of others, whether those of people, animals or trees. We feel for others. So, in this advanced state, advanced beyond the ordinary human, we cannot torture another person, because we would suffer the torture ourselves. One remembers Valentine's stigmata when I read to her of another's suffering. As for killing, what is the point, when one can psychically see the dead soldier arise from the body one has shattered?

The first stage, then, in this inter-communion with all nature, is the joyful awareness of one's own true spiritual group.

The best analogy of this inner working with a group incarnating on earth, is to imagine a circle of participants in group meditation. We are seated in the drawing-room of the Castle, and I am taking these people on a psychic trip. The curtains are drawn, incense sticks burning, and there are seven candles lighted. We have agreed on our area of shared projection: a beautiful grove of trees by the sea. So I describe the desired scene as vividly as I can, psychically projecting the scene as I speak. The stipulated time of silence is half-an-hour. I say that after this period of earth time, my voice will summon the astral travellers back to the drawing-room. So off we go. But I only half project, and keep an eye on the circle, to see how things are going.

The small group of astral tourists duly project to the woodland grove near the sea. Two members of the circle are fully on the spot, and are intelligently surveying the scene. Another, an intellectual, is day-dreaming, because he dislikes losing himself. Half of himself is in the drawing-room, and I am amused to note that he is watching me through one half-opened eye! He is suspicious of hypnosis. So he is half by the sea, half in the drawing-room - like myself.

Now, though the group locate themselves in the same area, in a grove of trees, they are apt to wander off on their own. Most of them, being seasoned travellers, make themselves happy and comfortable. Anyway, they are aware that this is a projected trip, and that they are to return at the right time, called by a Voice. Meanwhile, they pursue their various aims, whether studious, helpful or artistic.

But one of our tourists is a newcomer. He gets into difficulties. He not only loses himself in the grove of trees, but he loses himself also in the projection. He completely forgets that his greater self is seated in the Castle drawing-room!

He has an unpleasant time. I ask him what is happening, and he is able to tell me. He fights a duel with a dark man on a black horse. He attacks an upraised cobra. Not only this: he announces that one of his fellow travellers is evil, and that he is going to kill him. I realize that this person has become emotionally disturbed. Also that he is upsetting the young man next to him. I recollect that they were arguing over religion and politics, though in a friendly way, at lunch. So this was the outcome in the psychic sphere!

Do I leave them to sort it out? Or do I bring back the disturbed young man, at once?

In this case, I would play safe and bring everyone back straight away. Otherwise the unpleasant atmosphere might spread through the group.

I have later to explain to the young man who had been so aggressive, that he was not yet ready to work with us in trance state. But I might be able to help him on his own.

And here we have a reflection of what actually happens in that group dreaming that we call earthly life. So it is our business to learn to project in a wise and happy way in daily living. And, above all, not to forget that we dream. Otherwise we may lose contact with the Reality that the ignorant call non-existent; the wise, the World of Archetypes.

# CHAPTER 15

# THE TRAVELLER AT THE GATEWAY

ALL our essays so far have been trial runs: astral projection through trance, dream changing, and sporadic 'magnetic' happenings. These merely show a sign-post that there are other spheres of consciousness transcending our own. Finally, we have to learn to be able to ascend and descend the planes of being with conscious will. Otherwise we are the plaything of various forces, and have no power of choice. Travelling on the London underground system, one chooses one's destination; and one learns where to change trains, which moving stairway to use. So in learning to change one's level of being. one has to learn the rules for safe progress.

As usual, when we wish to learn how to do something that is new and strange, it is best to take simple instances in our every-day lives. Spending an evening in earth life, we can choose whom we shall meet, where to go, and what to do when we get there. The young people in the Castle can choose to walk down the avenue during the evening, and go to either of the two public houses in the village. Within one of these they can sing ballads, drink moderately or too much, argue, or make friends. Another of them can choose to stay in the Castle and play classical records. Someone else is busy writing a book in the library. A girl is making a dress. And others sit with me in group meditation. An older visitor has gone early to bed and is fast asleep.

So in our experiments with consciousness, it is of vital importance to choose where we want to go, what we want to do, and why. Otherwise we will not only waste time and energy, but may get lost.

For there is always that person who is led into spending an evening in an unpleasant way, and is left with a hangover from too much drinking, or a bad headache from excessive study.

It must be realized that though good may be termed absolute, the expression of the absolute in this earth life is relative to the person and circumstances. So ethics are absolute and of God: morality, what one chooses to do, is relative to one's spiritual age, one's natural talents, and one's particular path. I emphasise this because, when it comes to choice, one is not really free to criticise the way anyone else elects to spend his time. Sincerity is the most important thing. To sing ballads in the local public house, if one really likes it, is infinitely more worth-while than to sit through highbrow records as a duty, when really one is bored: Or to sit pretending to meditate, in order to feel spiritually superior to other people.

This relativity of choice also applies to a person's aspiration for heightened consciousness. It is easy to believe that it is good to ascend, to be 'up', and to visualize oneself joining the angels in heaven, but how sincere is one?

I once made up a ridiculous story of the Day of Judgement, in which angels suddenly appeared to humanity, and said that they were going to whisk the Do-gooders up to heaven! The unrighteous could stay behind on earth for many more lives, without any missionaries, welfare workers and the rest of the Righteous. The unrighteous were naturally extremely pleased at this, and announced at once that public houses would remain open all night, that censorship could go, and that now at last they were free to be happy in their own way. As they saw the Righteous whirl up to heaven in spaceships, they heartily thanked the angels; and looked forward to a cheerful future, having plenty of food, drink, sex and babies.

However, I could not picture the Righteous as being that pleased. They had been spending hours in churches singing about going to heaven, leaving behind all earthly fleeting pleasures, but now . . . did they like the prospect before them as they floated upwards? Never again would they feel the lash of rain and wind, to laugh, to eat, to drink, to make love. Never again could they argue and fight, gossip, or experience bodily pleasure. They could put up with such deprivations, if the Unrighteous were to suffer in hell. But to have to leave them inheriting the earth, actually enjoying themselves! This was too much.

What is this heaven like that you are taking us up to? They might well ask the angels. And the reply? Heaven is as you have portrayed it. You are expected to spend your time there singing psalms and playing the organ - in plainsong. Not even Gounod is allowed in such a heaven.

The punishment of the hypocrite is to receive what he pretends he likes. The fate of all snobs.

So when we determine that we want to increase our consciousness, we must first be sure that we really want to do this: and do not secretly yearn to go off and make money, or travel by jet-plane to some more earthly paradise. For to be half-minded in this matter is to lose both worlds, this one and the next.

As regards the motive, when I began studying these matters, I was at first much impressed by high-flown expressions of ideals. Now I have learnt to respect a genuine heart's desire however humble, rather than an elaborately worded expression of altruism. For it is not the surface mind that tells the truth, but the inner promptings of the soul. Some of the deepest people have the best sense of humour! Yes! I think that is my own personal criterion. A sense of humour and spiritual pride cannot co-exist.

I notice that the young are apt to rush into an attempt at mystical experience without any caution. They are sincere, yes: whole-hearted! But prudence is also needed. One takes one step at a time.

Once I told a cautionary tale on this subject, as a group of us sat under the Weeping Ash on the Castle terrace. It was a hot sunny August day, and it was my turn to give the morning's talk. But it was not a talking sort of day. In the distance was the hum of the lawn-mower bringing us the smell of newly cut grass. The birds were singing in the wilderness behind us, and the sun came through the light green ash leaves, making us drowsy. Still more distracting, Shep, our sheepdog, had joined us, jumping up and licking us . . . But I still wanted to convey an idea on evolving consciousness. So I asked to be inspired. This story came through

"There was a holy man who lived in the South of India," I said. "He belonged to that dark race who were inhabitants of the country centuries before the coming of the Four Castes. He sat naked under a palm tree. A group of disciples sat round him. His wisdom was suitable for their hearing; for he spoke of one-pointedness, of purity, of samadhi. He told of the all-pervading Self, and of the spark of that self within all creatures. When the disciples were dispersed, the Holy Man noticed that one lingered. This was a young student, the most intellectual of his disciples.

The young man said: 'Holy Guru, I have indeed been enlightened by your teachings. My heart is full of ecstasy. I am determined on a life of renunciation; and have already repudiated any thought of marriage. However, there is one thought that is darkening my mind. It is said that you hold a secret class at night! And I ask, what manner of pupils and what manner of teachings can come of darkness?'

Said the Holy One: 'My dear son; doubt is indeed darkness. I council you to banish all doubt from your mind. Think not of the night or what occurs there, and you will attain the light.'

But the young man was not so easily satisfied. His whole mind was now obsessed by the mystery of the secret class. Were great secrets being kept from him? He could not even meditate with propriety. A thousand conjectures tormented him. He had to find out.

So one evening he determined to hide himself in his Master's house, and uncover the mystery of the night. So when the Guru was saying his evening prayers by the sacred pool, the disciple hid himself behind a black carved chest in his Master's simple room.

Soon the Holy man entered the room, and sat on his deerskin mat in profound meditation. Nothing else happened for a few hours. Then, as the time grew towards midnight, the disciple felt his scalp crawl with terror. For something was oozing up from the earth floor. It was a creature of the darkness, furry, with orange eyes. To join him, there came from the rafters a green reptile with scales and eyes on stalks and eight legs, like no monster the quivering disciple had ever imagined could exist. Now there gambolled in little pink prickly things who giggled. These the disciple found particularly revolting, because they ran up and down the chest and turned somersaults on the floor.

Finally, this dreadful company was completed with the arrival through the earth of two demons with horns, one fat and thin; the other, round and chubby. They were accompanied by a very small purple dragon with bat-like wings, who appeared to be highly favoured, for he coiled about the Holy One's feet. Needless to say, none of this disturbed the Guru's meditation in the slightest. The disciple was terrified less the chattering of his teeth might be heard by this assembly of monsters, and that he should forthwith be devoured.

Now, at the appropriate time, the Guru began a lengthy and extremely erudite sermon on the all-pervading Self. It was on the lines of his morning's discourse; but more profound. The monsters listened with respectful attention. Not so the disciple, who was unable to benefit from the sublime truths so exquisitely elucidated. Finally his sufferings were mercifully ended by a deep swoon.

In the morning, when the Holy One had gone forth to bathe, the disciple managed to crawl out from behind the chest unobserved, and escape into the fresh air.

However, he now had acquired a facial twitch, a paralysed left arm; and his hair had gone white.

The Guru surveyed him kindly when he saw him lying by the pool 'My dear son,' he said; 'I observe that the Path is not yet for you.

'Always remember that to take two steps forward, it is wisest to take one backwards. Your father's farm has need of an additional worker.'

So the disciple went home to his father, and worked on the land. After all, he had gone to the Guru to learn. And he had learnt.

So I ended the story and it was time for us to help rake the grass off the lawn."

# CHAPTER 16

# THE MANY COLOURED PATTERN

IT was a fellow worker of ours, Natasha, who introduced me to a curious form of psychic faculty, 'microscopic clairvoyance.' This is different from usual clairvoyance. By tuning in to the etheric web, she was able to see, not only 'power', but the tiny swirling particles that formed the structure of all physical objects. Through focussing a concentration on the etheric structure, particularly above a human being's head, she could see what Yogananda calls 'Lifetrons', in his 'Autobiography of a Yogi'. After much practice I learnt to see these etheric atoms which are even smaller than electrons, positrons and neutrons. I saw them as colourless specks swirling like steam in violent agitation. This was not to be confused with 'ectoplasm,' a smoke-like vapour extruding from organic matter, which I had already learnt to see.

I brought this art back to the Castle, and found that the young people there had also this faculty latent in them. Indeed, Deirdre could see these Lifetrons at night, and said that when she saw those that composed her bedroom door, she could see right through her door into the room beyond.

Those more expert than myself saw Lifetrons in various colours. Thought would produce an explosion of Lifetrons from a person's head. I have watched a mystic in meditation: the top of his head looked opened up like a volcano, steaming with unregulated Lifetrons spurting in every direction!

One of the oddest discovery that Natasha made was to find archetypal forms within the matrix of 'atoms'. Indeed, she could see what was possibly the shape of things to come, born through mind. Curiously enough, the forms she saw within Lifetrons were of archetypal Greek style. Was it possible that human 'brain-waves' really contained germinal ideal forms, later to be translated into physical objects? One is reminded of children's comics, with cartoon people with bubbles of thought coming out of their heads, before transformation into words, expressed in balloons proceeding from their mouths!

The implications of this is tremendous. First comes the imagination: then comes the embodiment of that imaging right down through the planes of being, from the most refined to the coarsest. So here comes direct Creation.

So we can see that Deity is eternal, and has no beginning and no end. All that exists, humans, animals, plants, each element and atom, are individualized images of God. When it comes to creation, each mind-born creature can make his vehicle of consciousness, and in-breathe himself into his own creation. An Adept can create and insoul his own psychic body: he can also create a physical body through manipulation of lifetrons. He may astonish the ignorant by his ability to walk on water, pass through 'solid' walls, and raise his body from the dead. For we are all creative sons and daughters of God, but have forgotten this. The Master knows it.

When one considers the fantastic explosion produced by the fission of one uranium atom, one has some conception of the meaning of occult power. And why also the development of this power is only entrusted into the custody of Initiates. Evolution proceeds instinctively from mineral to plant, from plant to animal: but for man evolution becomes a co-operation with the Gods. We ourselves have to take the necessary step from 'Homo Sapiens' to Spiritual Man.

It is here that we so often fail. For arrogance of our species leads us to suppose that the Superman is a domineering, power-loving creature who imposes his authority on the rest of life. But this is the exact opposite from the true Adept. The first step to expanding our consciousness is to have sympathy with the feelings of everyone and everything else. Otherwise we merely specialize in being ourselves. And to specialize is to involve, to involute. The path of evolution is to spread our interests, our abilities, our love, to include more and more of awareness of the whole of life. This detachment from personal identification brings one to the Spiritual sphere of consciousness that includes the lesser levels.

Fiona, Angela and I formed a group for attaining expanded consciousness. Angela had a useful knowledge of philosophy; Fiona, psychic and spiritual clairvoyance, and I could bring through power needed for working directly on consciousness.

The most remarkable discovery we made for ourselves was that consciousness is multiple, and manifests on many planes at the same time. It was Angela who brought through this multi-consciousness.

I remember particularly her vision of the Hall of the Western Orders. She was lying on a couch in Fiona's London house, and I was taking notes. Fiona was using her clairvoyant faculty to see what was happening.

When Angela had attained the psychic or 'astral' level of consciousness, she announced that she was going into a deeper state of awareness - into the 'mental' or spiritual sphere. Her report while in this state was lucid and without pause for half-an-hour, and I took notes all the time. She described herself as being in a mighty hall, with stained-glass windows along the sides. In the place of honour was the symbol of the White Dove. She was able to describe each of the stained-glass windows in detail: each one represented a Western Order. I remember particularly her account of the window of the Order of the Garter. I have never thought this Order had any but purely social and ceremonial importance.

The inner meaning of the Order, she said, was of a beggar being taken up into heaven, and given a glass of wine. This struck me as being appropriate. There was said to be a link with the Order of the Garter and the old religion of Witchcraft. Of all the Western Orders this would be the most practical, because the most universal, for today. Imagine a board of Directors with the great Queen Elizabeth, Charles II, and Lord Chesterfield on the council! The cultural level would be high, and the knowledge of wordly matters broad.

As these thoughts flashed through my mind, I noticed that Angela was not particularly interested in this Order, or the others she was describing. She was looking for something.

"I cannot find it," she said. "It is not here."

"What?"I asked.

"The Order of the Temple,"she replied. "There is no window for the Knights Templar."

When she returned from trance, I read back her own report. Angela was amazed.

"This is completely different to what happened!" She said. At first she seemed to doubt my words, until Fiona confirmed my report, and I showed my writing. Her words had filled a full half-an-hour.

But Angela, during the space of this same half-an-hour had, she said, been somewhere completely different; in a mountain landscape. There she had discovered a shrine devoted to the Order of the Temple: The Order, she said, had had an ideal too high for earth life. Its inner aim was represented by the Madonna of the Immaculate Conception. Not the Madonna with a child.

This referred to direct birth from Divine mind of the Santa Sophia, heaven-born wisdom. This, the third aspect of the Trinity, was the Holy Spirit. It entered from the highest, and so descended to the lowest, so bringing about Direct Creation. Qabalistically, this typified 'Kether to Malkuth.' It represented a descent from the Crown Centre, 'Atma', to the lowest centre of Kali at the base of the spine. I could see that the very height of this ideal could lead to a split in consciousness, because it left out the middle centres, heart and plexus, the emotions of the 'astral' or psychic sphere. I reflected that the Order of the Garter, with its blue sash, the girdle of Venus, running from shoulder, across the heart to the hip, remedied this division. It would not be a celibate Order, not so high as the Order of the Temple, but had lasted longer on the physical earth. It was rooted on the Stone of Destiny.

However, one thing struck the three of us. We had been dealing with three aspects of Angela's consciousness. She had reported to me coherently, choosing her words with care, as she always did. A stranger might not have realized she was in trance. But she said she had no knowledge in her trance of our present-day existence, save for a voice - not recognized as that of Olivia - that kept asking her questions. Indeed, she said, if she had not replied at once to this voice, she would have forgotten modern life altogether!

But her report on the Hall of the Western Orders had been so vividly described, that I had no doubt that another part of herself had been there, during the half-hour of trance.

However, she declared that during that same period of time 'she' had been entirely involved in walking around a mountain landscape; and she could remember every detail. That which was missing from her report to me - the window of the Order of the Temple - was experienced by another part of herself in a shrine within this landscape.

The three of us pieced together what we thought had happened. The Greater Self, which we can call 'X', had many facets and many 'bodies': but the main focus in this experience had been on the psychic level, within a landscape. This was remembered through that part of 'X' called Angela, a present-day woman. However, on a higher level, another part of 'X' as projected into the Mental Sphere. This, being spiritual, could not be brought through to Angela's physical brain.

And for all we knew, there were still more facets of 'X' existing in still more levels of being. So we had to postulate that 'X' was greater than Angela, greater than anyone else she may have been in past lives, because it included all the multi-patterned facets that made up her spirit.

The clue for us then lay in the fact that the Greater Consciousness was there all the time. We did not have to seek it, fight for it, restrict ourselves for it. It was a question of spiritual realization. And, paradoxically, this realization was pleasant and natural. Transcending passing time, it contained the past, present and even the future within its spectrum.

Once one could contact one's true self, all the rest came easily. One had much more life, not less. We were like people imprisoned in one little room, suddenly faced with the freedom of a whole beautiful house; and a glimpse of a garden through the windows. The Temple of the Stars had been around us all the time.

*Etherial silver or gold streams of power can be seen by some occult students and psychics spreading like antlers from the head.*

# CHAPTER 17

# THE COSMIC SPIRAL

ANGELA once told us in a deep trance she had discovered the Mystery of the Universe! She was determined to bring this knowledge back to benefit the world. So she memorized two words that explained the Great Mystery. As she came back from trance, she uttered these two words: 'Cherry-Tart.'

And she could remember no more.

So this then is the problem of the mystic: how to bring back his knowledge through his physical brain. The three of us, Angela, Fiona and I, had further enlightenment on the subject during one particular trance session. The final result could be described as a little more explicit than 'Cherry-Tart.' As usual, I was acting as Operator, Fiona, as clairvoyant, and Angela was Trance Percipient.

Angela on this occasion reported that she was ascending into 'the higher Mental Plane', the sphere of Causes: here, she said, were the shining archetypes of existence. She described aerial white forms of lions and children and birds and fish, amidst sparkling fountains and snowy gardens, not yet with individuality and protective colouring. Here was the World of the Unborn.

She said that she was facing a great rose-coloured Light. She entered into this Light and felt a feeling of joy and love. Within the rose-coloured Light was a golden brightness. Into this she entered, and experienced spiritual glory. Finally, within the golden Light, came pure White Light.

"I enter within the pure White Light," she said; "and I see a chalice upheld by two hands. Within the chalice is a violet Radiance; and within this radiance I see the form of a city about to be born. I see its white towers and domes and its shining streets and gardens. And I hear a voice saying: 'Love comes not only from Two, but from Three.'"

And here Angela gradually returned from her exalted state of consciousness.

I was much impressed by this report, and after the session asked for her own account of what had happened.

"Well," she said; "I was having a nice time in a beautiful landscape. Then I began to go up, and saw my body sitting there below. When I got up into the sky, I saw a lot of white shiny creatures including a tiny white horse, and children playing about in clouds, throwing Power around in a game. Then I saw a huge pink rose. I went into the rose, and there was another rose, a yellow one inside it. I went into that and found a white rose in the middle. That is all I can remember. I then floated down, saw my body in the landscape and entered it, and I came down into my body here."

If one substitutes 'Cherry Tart' for red, yellow and white roses, one gets the problem. The most sublime experiences are almost impossible to bring back to physical consciousness. All that remains is an analogous description. In this case one notices that radiant lights are embodied as coloured roses. So the mystic, on return, translates the ineffable experience of his spirit, into language understood by his soul and brain. He will transform what he cannot understand into the sacred symbols of his particular religion and philosophy. As for the highest vision of all, Angela had no memory of the mystic Chalice or of the creation of the archetypal city.

Participation is a key word for the future. We can add Creativity and Universality. We notice that the perfect city is first created by the symbiosis of Three in the world of Archetypes: and then is relayed through to the sphere of our physical world. One day we will ourselves participate in direct creation, and help to build the forms to be animated by Universal Spirit. We can learn to give birth, not only to our children, but to ideal worlds.

I myself was once able to bring through knowledge gained from an experience of cosmic consciousness. I saw Life emerging from That which was beyond light and darkness, containing all within Itself. There was all time in its matrix, all beings latent within itself.

Then I saw this Unity involve itself in a spinning movement, the direction from right to left, until it had divided itself into Seven. This Seven I saw personified in the form of seven Cosmic Deities. They were associated with certain colours and characteristics. I myself saw them as Gods, but I knew they could equally well be seen as Goddesses. I was given to understand that I was not to identify these Seven only with the planets of our solar system. Our particular system was a microcosm of a greater universe: nonetheless there was a relationship with the Great Seven and our particular planets.

I felt happiest with the first Deity, whom one could equate with Mars, Aries, and Dionysus. His colours were scarlet and gold. These Powers were reflected in a reverse aspect on earth. I recognised that people like Goethe and Napoleon were associated with this first archetype: also the concept of Christ the King.

The second Deity was clearly identifiable with the God Phoebus Apollo. The colours were green and silver. Buddha and Beethoven seemed to be connected with this.

The third God I liked very much. He was associated with Hermes, and was accompanied with the colour blue. I suppose you could say its reverse aspect on earth would be 'Mercury' and be the contrary colour - orange. The good of this great Power appeared to lie in pure contemplation.

The middle Deity's colour was a brilliant green, and could be related to the word 'Jove' - Jovial! It seemed to be connected with many writers like Dickens and H. G. Wells, who had a multitude of strange and diverse characters in their works - the more the merrier. In fact this Power generated a multiplicity of forms.

The fifth God, I was told, was the easiest to remember. This Power could be called quite clearly, 'Saturn'. The Prophet Muhammed could be associated with this, and such people as the Emperor Vespasian, Jonathan Swift, and Abraham Lincoln. They all had the same look, and said the same sort of things!

The sixth and seventh Deities terrified me. The sixth could be called 'Uranus', and I identified the music of Bach with him. This Power dealt with Time, and things coming back on themselves in cycles.

The seventh was violet in colour, and I associated it with Leonado de Vinci. I was told that in reverse aspect, this power could induce people to try and create on their own, without the other Seven, which led to sterility.

Naturally, I wanted to know how these Powers created the Seven Universes that came from them. It involved the merging of all Seven through blending radiations. I cannot describe this process, except that it filled me with unspeakable awe. When all Seven were One, I was told that from the Heart of Love all creation came forth, from Gods and Goddesses, to humans, animals, caterpillars! Every single blade of grass, every atom.

When the time came for all these Universes to come back again into Unity, having enjoyed being their separated selves for a while, everything began to join up again, this time revolving from left to right, faster and faster.

The descent and ascent of manifestation I was shown as Power forming itself into spirals. The macrocosmic spiral when involution took place, involved itself into lesser spirals. as Power descended through the spheres. It was as if the spirals were pulled inside out, through themselves, like that game we call cats' cradles played with string.

Evolution took the opposite form: the spirals expanded into still greater ones, until they joined the universe that came from the Gods: and then the Gods themselves re-joined the Unmanifested Unity: Cosmic Night.

What formed the spirals in the first place was Time, the adjustment from past to present. When time folded up on itself, the spirals became rings of light, and then entered into the One.

It was only some years after receiving this mystical experience, that I read books about 'Seven Rays', and other occult teachings. I received my visions directly from my own expanded consciousness; but was also decidedly taught by Spirit Intelligences. I was shown coloured pictures as if I were a child of five. And I felt like that, ignorant. And I still do.

The main impression left on my mind is that thought, feeling and imagination are expressed through time, expansion and speed. As one thinks and feels and imagines more and more profoundly, in some extraordinary way this manifests through acceleration of speed, increase of size and the telescoping of time.

In this case, if one were to meditate sufficiently deeply, one might alter one's rate of speed, time and size. From this could come levitation, even teleportation! One might even find oneself in another universe.

After all, we may be able to connect the 'level' and 'sphere' of the mystic, to the word 'universe' as used by the scientist. There seem to be universes within universes. The scientific theory of Infinite Complexity appears to be approaching the truth!

This is not far beyond us, because we each one of us are a microcosm of the Whole. We carry the Stars about our head, bestowing on us the perception of Truth in any form, including the capacity to see a joke! We have the Solar Sphere warm in our hearts, when we love, or even feel in a friendly mood. And certainly we are familiar with the Earth-Moon of instincts and our physical bodies.

What we are trying to do nowadays is not only to aspire to the stars: to have religious devotion in the heart: but to respect the emotional and physical plane on which we have to work. This is, curiously enough, the hardest task. Most of us have wondered at the fantastic difference between the divine Gothic art, and the cruel medieval penal code and appalling social conditions. We have been awed by Greek thought, and revolted by their treatment of those whom they called 'slaves' and 'barbarians'.

So it is our present task to bridge the gap between the Ideal and the actual. The mystic, returning from greater consciousness, need not necessarily join a monastery or convent. Rather now may he become a doctor, a politician, or a scientist.

Having undergone the Initiations of the Moon and the Sun, and experienced the apotheosis of the Stars, our next step is to return to earth. For it is on the earth that our help is needed. We can truly now make it a happier place for humans, animals and plants. Angela saw roses in heaven. We can learn to see all the heavens in a rose.

*A city about to be born*

# CHAPTER 18

# COMING DOWN TO EARTH

I HAD a friend who thought he was God. He came to this conclusion during a mystical revelation. However, what made him particularly irritating to his friends was that he was not only God, but the only God.

To effect a cure, his long-suffering friends got hold of a witch who had had a similar mystical opening. Left alone with our friend, she managed to convince him that she too was God.

But this spoilt it for him. To share his Godhead with a witch - and a female at that! Speedily he came down to earth.

It is the return journey from mystical awakening and religious revelation that brings about the greatest dangers. There is the risk of misinterpretation, hence fanaticism, on the part of the Prophet and Visionary; a separation from the rest of humanity through spiritual isolation. And, most upsetting from a planetary point of view, possible mental and emotional unbalance affecting both spiritual leader and his followers.

It appears to me that myths of the past may really present present-day actuality. Are we Atlanteans, about to lose ourselves in a deluge of our own creation? Are we the legendary planet 'Maldek' destroyed by misused power? We foolish humans steal the forbidden apples of Eden and, through our scientific technology, hope to be as gods, when we lack the ethical qualifications for godhead! And as a consequence, we are poisoning a third of the seas, a third of the vegetation, a third part of the air, as prophesised in the Book of Revelations.

Once a story came to me on this subject. I told it in the Temple of Isis, and three musicians accompanied my narration with flute, mandolin and organ. Rosalind took the part of the little girl: Helena of the Devi.

"Once upon a time," I said, "there was a strange little planet that had a roof around it, like a large plastic umbrella. For the people there did not care for weather changes, and preferred to live with regulated illumination and heating. They preferred artificial flowers and plants: and instead of real live animals, they liked 'Cosi-Pets', artificially made animals and birds that were both hygenic and non-reproductive. Foodstuffs and plants came likewise from computerised factories.

However, there was one odd small girl who lived in a weird island to the West of this planet. She was so peculiar that when she was alone she took off her pretty face-mask and her all-over tights: and she would dance all on her own with a naked face and body, on a neglected piece of waste pavement.

You may ask why was anything waste on this efficient planet? But the inhabitants of the Western island were negligent and they had neglected to keep their bit of the sky-umbrella mended! So it leaked. Naturally people avoided the leak. So that bit of pavement became neglected.

But the little girl enjoyed playing with the leak, and liked its cold splashiness more than her hot sanitary cosi-bath provided by the Municipality.

Now in the place of the leak, owing to the continual dripping, came about a crack on the pastel plasti-floor that covered the whole planetery surface. And in this crack exuded a dreadful stuff called 'earth'. It became still more shocking when it got wet through the leak, for then it became 'mud'. Of course the authorities would have made the Sani-squad clean up this at once. However, up to now the leak had not been reported to the Municipality. As for the little girl, she liked mud! She made pies with it.

Then the most extraordinary thing began to happen. The only living plant on the planet began to show its green head. Up and up it grew, and the little girl loved it. It was her only friend and she used to converse with it.

However, a crisis came in her short life. Her peculiarity had not gone unnoticed by the local Sub-teenage Psychiatrist. Her habit of not wearing her pretty face-mask, secretly removing her all-over tights, and above all, an atavistic tendency to sing and dance, plainly indicated that she was retarded. Her foster-mother in her commune was told that the child would have to go into an Institution for the socially maladjusted.

However, the little girl was so socially maladjusted that she did not want to co-operate with her psychiatrist. She determined to escape. So she marched off to her plant, which was a bean-stalk, and had by now grown right through the planetary roof. And she asked the plant to help her.

This was Helena's cue to appear with appropriate music. She appeared as the Beanstalk Devi, and offered to take the girl up the plant into the air above.

At this point I used to vary the ending. There was our natural desire to bring the plasti-dome down on to the unattractive inhabitants of this planet, along with their tinted facemasks, their cuddly cosi-pets, and plastic plants! The more humane ending was to transport the girl to a better place, from whence she could return when grown-up and, with new. friends from the sky, help to release the pallid wretches in their self-created prison.

These stories are best left open, because the imagination can truly create when left its own freedom. As we dream today, we live tomorrow.

Yes, but can the little girl really return from another sphere and bring back her experience of a better life? Such a girl in the past might have been incarcerated in convent, prison or madhouse. Anyway, she would have been socially unacceptable. No race likes its successors.

At present, for the first time for many hundreds of years, a new race of mystics may reveal themselves without persecution. It is as if human mutation is at last taken place. Those who take drugs only provide cover for true visionaries: those who are born with faculties that need no drugs for their manifestation.

What happens now? We have a bizarre situation, in which one lot of people, the majority of the race, 'Homo Sapien', still ruling the planet, are puzzled by a new race of weird creatures appearing among them; their own children, but with a different appearance, language and habits! And these oddities claim to be creating an alternative society: a society they believe will supersede the old establishment. And these gentle people with long hair, soft voices and strange beliefs, are manifesting in all countries, making old-fashioned creeds, whether religious or Marxist, seem irrelevant.

It is easy to sympathise with ordinary men and women faced with weird progeny. But what of the point of view of the 'mutants'?

To take an example. A young man has had a mystical opening, which he calls 'being blissed out of his head.' How does he relate to others who have not had a similar experience? He may suffer acutely from the psychological clash.

I once experienced just such an agonizing clash when I was in a heightened state of consciousness, with others who were not. They happened to be talking about fishing! I felt tortured psychically. This state lasted for about three minutes. I do not think I could have endured it any longer.

These experiences are not always horrific in relation to daily physical life. Once I was able to see the divine correspondence in all about me. I knew the spiritual significance of hedges, of grass, of the points of the compass. I was able to see a shining good in people and animals, masked by outer personality. It was outer personality that gave the impression that all about me were in a sleep.

One realizes the relativity of this, because as I descended from the ecstatic state, everyone else became 'awake' again.

It was only years later that I met others who had had similar experiences. Natasha said that in this state of greater consciousness, all the world shone with glory, and even the cat smiled at her! Another man, a scientist, said that as he was walking along Lincoln's Inn fields, he attained this cosmic consciousness. It was cosmic, because he was one with all that was. He said he met a Down-and-Out, and he knew that he had only to say one word to this tramp, and so great was his power that he could have transformed the whole of the man's life. But, over-awed by this tremendous force working through him, my friend prayed that he might return to his usual diminished state of selfishness:- at this, the power left him.

It was only at the end of the sixties that I realized that these spontaneous mystical experiences were becoming widespread. They seem to be 'catching'. If you are in a room with a person in this state of euphoria you can, through the telepathic network, pick up the condition.

Now one can see the problem for those who not only have had one or two mystical experiences, but, as the young graphically put it, are usually 'high', having had their 'minds blown' . Imagine a London street, in which men and women rush to and fro in what we call a normal state of consciousness. And among these ordinary citizens some weird creatures saunter, 'turned on'. Add to these pleasant dreamers others with criminal tendencies, opened up dangerously through drugs, and you have the present day scene.

The best thing to do is to give advice to those who find themselves unexpectedly opened up psychically, owing possibly to a vegetarian diet, the practice of meditation, and the reading of occult books.

Learning to discriminate between the various spheres is the most important safeguard. For instance, a girl leaves her group meditation session, and at first is happy as she sails down the local high-street, her mind over-flowing with universal love and good-will. Suddenly, frighteningly, she is assailed by all the worries, the miseries and frustration of those in the high-street: also she feels the suffering of animals, as she passes a butcher's shop. For in this state she does not see a piece of dead meat, but the whole animal that once grazed in green pastures. She must learn to keep her revulsion to herself. Already a policeman is eyeing her suspiciously.

Then she sees an encouraging notice high up on a wall: 'Take Courage'. She feels joyful. Angels have put it there in lights. . .She fails to notice that she is looking at an advertisement for ale!

Then she is afraid. Glaring at her on the back of a red bus she is assailed by the menacing words: 'Watch your Step!' She takes this to be a threat from Dark Forces, and does not realize that she is reading a warning to jay-walkers from London Transport. . . In fact she acts so strangely that she may eventually end up in a mental hospital.

The psychiatric diagnosis of schizophrenia is only too accurate: she had been experiencing two levels of consciousness in the wrong place, at the wrong time: hence deriving no benefit from either.

It would seem then that psychics would do well to treat themselves with the same care they pay to a television set, and make sure what channel they are on! If any. And this requires not only well-balanced emotion, but a state of mental development brought about by natural brain capacity and a good education. Occult knowledge could not have been given in the Middle Ages to the mass of people, because they were intellectually under-developed.

Only now, with general education, is there the possibility of a big step forward by humanity into greater spiritual consciousness.

When one surveys the condition of the earth, threatened by global war, planetary pollution, the possibility of a beautiful change dawning on earth seems remote! But the physical world is created through the action of mind; and the mind is capable of fantastic change when its environment is threatened.

I myself find it heartening to reflect that the vision of the two Initiations, of Water and of Fire, have already been given to us at the end of the nineteenth and the beginning of the twentieth century. When a Mystery is performed on the earth before an earthly audience, a new age is upon us. Studying the Eleusinian mysteries of Demeter and Persephone, to me the visions of Lourdes and Fatima are a portrayal of these dramas in actual human history.

The Lesser Mystery was shown at Lourdes in the form of a vision of a beautiful maiden appearing in a grotto. The young girl who witnessed the visions drew forth a stream of healing water from the mud.

The Greater Eleusinian mystery was, I believe, manifested at Fatima. Here we have people seeing a Golden Disc bringing from the sky the apparition of a woman robed in white. The visions were shown to three children, and occurred on each thirteenth of the month, from May to October; so including the ancient dates of the Mysteries of the Goddesses. At the culmination in October, seventy thousand onlookers saw a sun disc revolve, and show spectroscopic change: they called it 'the dancing sun'.

The Lesser Mystery of Lourdes therefore, portrayed Persephone, Queen of Day and Night, the perfect embodiment of a Divine Idea, in control of the elements of Earth and Water. The Greater Mystery of Fatima illustrated power over the elements of Air and Fire. So unseen Teachers demonstrate in visionary drama the symbols of positive and negative forces. Water and Fire unite: Sun and Moon are one. In other parts of the world, through various religions, the same message is being given to us. There is need of harmony between East and West: Mind and Heart. From the uniting of opposites comes creativity.

How can we as individuals co-operate with this great work? It is best, I feel, for like-minded people to combine into meditation circles. No special temple is needed: any room may be used in a friend's house. And for private daily meditation, one can set aside even a corner of a room for one's spiritual attunement with Divinity.

And through this habitual focussing of awareness, inspiration will come. Of course inspiration varies with each one of us: one may surprise oneself by developing an unexpected talent. Instead of specializing in one particular form of work or gift, one may discover pleasure in painting, writing, singing, dancing and modelling clay: and one need not mind about a lack of proficiency!

To evolve spiritually, it is essential to extend one's field of awareness. Once inhibiting self-consciousness is cast aside, latent talents may flower gloriously.

As a growth of consciousness takes place, small groups join larger ones, who tend to seek a beautiful area in which to live together. In such centres humans live in harmony with animals, birds, trees and plants, with the spirit of Nature Herself. A network of such centres may bring about a wonderful transformation of our earth. For in the depth of each one of us is a longing to live happily with all that springs from the source of Divine Life.

Life does not limit itself to form or time or space. It is eternal, ever-conscious, all-pervading. In unity with this, we realize the joy of immortality, and are in harmony with all that is.

# Guide to Photographs

1.

2

3

5

6

7

8

9

10

11

12

13

14

15

# HISTORY OF
# CLONEGAL CASTLE

# LAWRENCE DURDIN-ROBERTSON

IN the South-East of Ireland between the Wicklow Mountains and the Blackstair Range, there flow two rivers. The main one is the Slaney. It rises a few miles above Baltinglass, passes through that town, Tullow, Bunclody and Enniscorthy, then flows into the sea at Wexford. A smaller river, the Derry, rising near Tinahely, passes through Shillelagh, Clonegal, then about one and a half miles below Clonegal joins the Slaney. The triangular area enclosed by them upstream from the meeting, is the "Macha" or "Crow's foot".

From the Macha as far as Dublin, was primeval forest. The area including Clonegal was known as the Leveroch. Traces of the primeval forest are believed to remain today - (Legends of Mount Leinster, Patrick Kennedy p.29) "As they descended a wild and broken road, through the gap of Coppenagh, they took little notice of the broad and high extent of the side of White Mountain, with its dark streaks of bog, its grey rocks and the primeval forest clothing its lower eminences." - in Ballyredmond Wood, in a small area on the right bank of Slaney known as "Ryans Rock", at Altamont, and part of some of the oak woods of the Coollattin Estate, and in the name of the Derry (grove of oak trees), and in that of Shillelagh - this being a form of bludgeon.

A Scottish story, told recently by Mr. White relates that a certain Scottish Chieftain, wounded at Culloden, was told by a wise woman that he would find healing (*slainte*) if he went to a place between the river of Health and the river of the Oak Tree. It is told that he was healed in the Slaney - Derry triangle, and so he may have stayed at Clonegal Castle.

A tradition related by Mr. Manning Robertson records how a Mrs. Benson, at the time of the flood, seeing the water rise, moved to higher ground; as she began to climb Mount Leinster (2,600 feet), Noah sailed by her in the Ark. Mrs. Benson called to Noah, "It's a soft day". "It is indeed" replied Noah. "Is there any room in your Ark for me?" she asked. "There is not", answered Noah, and then sailed away. Meanwhile Mrs. Benson had reached the top. As the waters still rose, she took some stones and threw them into a heap, forming the cairn, still to be seen.

The district known as the Leveroch remained unconquered during the time of Henry II, and Richard still did not subdue it; probably for that reason, he gave it to the Irish. It was part of the lands of the Clonmullen sept of the Kavanaghs. (Legends of Mount Leinster p.122) "It is about the Old Castle of Clonmullin on the valley that the Clody runs through, before it reaches the town. This old castle and the lands about it belonged of old to the noble and royal Family of the O'Kavanaghs". Then, Elizabeth conquered it, and gave it to the Netterville family who later, in 1615, sold it to the Esmondes. She destroyed three Kings' Castles including Clonogan Castle, which defended the Derry. Clonogan Castle was later known as Clonegal Castle (Field of the Stranger), it was rebuilt by Lord Esmonde, created the first baron Limbrick, as a fort for soldiers, under the command of Dudley Cocclough. Its dimensions (40 feet x 60 feet) with a semicircular tower at the back (S.W. side) are exactly those laid down by James I for keeping the land of that area.

It was started in 1625 taking 5 years to complete. It is built of local granite and quartz and built on a batter, the walls 6 foot thick at the bottom, 4 feet on the first floor, and 3 foot 6 inches at the top. Probably it had a thatched roof, just as nearby Carnew Castle, built in 1580, was known to be thatched. The original castle had five floors, unpartitioned, the basement including the Old Kitchen, with a very wide fireplace, the dungeon, and the Druid well. The first floor, including the Hall and the Drawing Room; the second floor, including the Blue, and Green, rooms and Stair Head Rooms, the third floor included the Red and Yellow, the White Rooms, the Mount Leinster Rooms, and the Red Room dressing room, the top floor consisting of the Attic, high enough to hold one fair sized bedroom.

Lord Esmonde married an Irish lady, Ellice (Eilis) O' Flaherty, grand-daughter of Grace O' Malley (Grainne Mhaoil), the well-known hereditary Queen of Connaught, a rival of Elizabeth. Lord Esmonde, being a Protestant, had his marriage annulled on the grounds of her being "mere Irishry" and his son Thomas by Eilis O' Flaherty was therefore illegitimate, and so the baronial title died out. Lady Esmonde's ghost is seen in the "Spy Bush" at the end of Back Avenue, where she watched for the return of her husband. She combs her hair in the moonlight, accompanied by a white cat; and the tradition holds that there are always white cats at the Castle. Subsequently he married a lady from the Butler family, leaving no issue.

One of the tasks given to Lord Esmonde was to survey that part of Ireland and to map out "The County of Wicklow" from Dublin, Carlow and Wexford. A map in the Castle shows the original counties of Dublin, Carlow and Wexford, before Wicklow county was delineated. Lord Esmonde was in the siege of Duncannon and died on his way back to Clonegal, in 1646.

Cromwell's troops, under Colonels Reynolds and Hewson went through the country and at the ford of the Derry defeated the Irish at the battle of Clonegal: the site of the battle is said to be at Kilcarry. The castle was taken by them; but we know that a bill for the men who had stayed there was sent in earlier.

Charles Topham Bowden recalls the first stanza of an old Ballad:-
> *"The sun of thy glory forever is set*
> *Ill-fated Hibernia in darkness profound*
> *With the blood of thy heroes Kilcarry is wet*
> *Desolation and death roam at large all around.*
> *The streams of old Derry which silver was called*
> *By the sweet bards of Orchard in happier days*
> *Are tainted with murders and crimsoned with gore*
> *Choked up with carnage and stopped in their way"*.

The son of Lord Esmonde, Thomas, left for France and joined Charles II and was made a baronet. Sir Thomas' son, Sir Laurence, returned in 1680 and turned his castle into his residence. He added the partitions between the rooms dividing the various floors. He panelled the Drawing-room and Dining-room and put in a carved granite fireplace in the Blue Room. He also built on the porch in 1680. He roofed the Castle in slates, slightly lowering it. Also in

1680, he planted the Front Avenue mainly with lime trees which came from France, and also the lime trees bordering the "Esmonde fish ponds" and the Mill pond above the haggard. The name of the castle was changed about then. Sir Laurence Esmonde married Lucy Kavanagh, thus uniting with the old owners of the district.

The castle was formerly known as Clonogan or Clonegal Castle, but was renamed about then Huntington Castle after a place called Hunnington in Lincolnshire from which the Esmondes originally came. The name "Huntington" probably was due to a mispronunciation. It was changed back to its old name of Clonegal Castle in the 1970s.

Sir Lawrence possibly built on part of the Kitchen wing. The ceiling of the Kitchen was restored in 1989, and on a rafter on the hall side was carved the date 1678. The present Red Room at the top of the castle, was used as a chapel. In Sir John Esmonde's time his brother, Richard, accidentally shot himself with a fowling-piece. The bullet mark is still to be seen about two feet up from the ground, in the panelling to the left of the pair of front doors.

In 1758 Sir John Esmonde died, leaving a widow, Eleanor and three daughters, Helen, Lucy and Isabella, but no sons. The castle was left to the daughters and the title passed to Sir Walter of another branch of the family. It was then decided to put the castle to auction because Eleanor's brother had a mortgage on it. It was valued by Charles Frizell; and was sold in 1758.

Lewis, in his Topographical Dictionary of Ireland (1838) describes thus the parish of Moyacomb or Clonegal:-

"Partly in the barony of Shillelagh, county of Wicklow, partly in that of Scarawalsh, county of Wexford, but chiefly in that of St. Mullins, county of Carlow and province of Leinster, on the road from Tullow to Newtown barry, and on the river Derry; containing with the post-town of Clonegal, and the village of Johnstown, 4877 inhabitants. It comprises 28,204 statute acres aplotted under the tithe act, includes the estate of Abbeydown, containing 452 plantation acres, which has been tithe-free from time immemorial and is considered extra parochial. The soil is varied, and there are some patches of bog. The state of agriculture is improving. A slate quarry has recently been opened on Gibbet Hill, near Johnstown. It is under a station of the constabulary police and contains an old castellated mansion of the Esmonde family. The Church, in the town of

Clonegal, is a good modern building, erected in 1819 for which the late Board of First Fruits granted a loan of £1,300, and the Ecclesiastical Commissioners recently granted £186 for its repair. There is a meeting house for Methodists at Clonegal. At Abbeydown are the remains of an Ancient Religious House, of which no account is extant". A sketch map of the Castle was found among some deeds dated 1758. It showed a pediment but no other additions to the main block; the Avenue trees were shown on it.

The highest bidder James Leslie, Bishop of Limerick, was declared the purchaser at £2,000. It is told that while he lived there, the balusters on the first and second flight of stairs did not extend as far as the stair, the last of the treads having no baluster. The Bishop tripped at this place and a newel-post of mahogany was put there; it is now known as the "Bishop's Post". He appears as a ghost in the four-poster bedroom standing to the left of the fireplace.

The eldest of the three Esmonde sisters Helen married in 1754, a Richard Durdin, and his brother Alexander rented the Castle and Estate on a three lives lease, £117 a year, and in 1828 he rented the estate from the Hon. Mrs. Halliburton, a niece of Bishop James Leslie. Alexander Durdin died in 1807 and left it to his widow and four sons; the youngest son, William, bought out the leasehold from his three brothers. "As the castle was greatly out of repair", £200 was remitted out of the rent, Alexander contracting to pay that amount on repairing the Castle and its outbuildings.

Alexander Durdin married four times (1) Miss Duncomb, (2) Mary Duncan, (3) Mrs. Anne Penn. Being a lawyer, Alexander was called in to make a will for Mrs. Penn. He asked her: "Why not marriage settlements"? They were married, and she died 3 weeks later. Mrs. Penn was the widow of the grandson of William Penn, founder of Pennsylvania. The miniature of the grandfather of this William Penn is in the possession of David Durdin-Robertson. The Penn family started a Law suit, which lasted 40 years; as a result, the Penns were given the American property, while the Irish property went to the Durdins. On Manning Robertson's marriage in 1912 the Penn-Gaskells gave him a mahogany tea-caddy fitted with cut glass, saying "It was to end a quarrel which lasted 150 years". Alexander's 4th marriage was to Barbara St. Leger descended from Sir William St. Leger, Lord Deputy of Munster (1627). A miniature of him, painted by Laurence Crosse in 1680, is in the possession of David Durdin-Robertson.

By Barbara, Alexander had 14 children; he died in 1807. He also built the battlements of bricks and plaster.

Bowden, travelling through all Ireland, describes the Castle thus:

"Huntington is likewise contiguous to poor Clonegal. Here is the delightful seat of Mr. Durdin, which commands a very extensive prospect. A superb avenue leads from this to Clonegal. The exuberant branches of the venerable trees at either side form a shade through which neither the sun, rain or wind can penetrate".

William Leader, Alexander's eldest son planted Scots Pine along the edge of the Bush meadow, along the Chapel field and also around the rath on which stands the Protestant Church. Being a medical doctor, he is believed to have attended people in the Famine; he died soon afterwards in 1849.

William Leader's son, Alexander (second) came into possession in 1849. He built on, in 1860, the Tapestry Room and the Library above it, and the Tower Room including the Tiled passage, the Pillar room (previously the pantry and scullery), the housekeepers' room and the room over the Potato house, also the Red house (cow byre and corn loft) and the pigsties. Up to 1884 the courtyard (S.W. of house) had a wall running diagonally from north to south, which supported a row of hen-houses and pigsties. With the buildings in the farmyard, the mounting block was left and still stands. Outside, he made the terraces, installed electric light in 1888, built the weir and turbine house with head race. It was the second house in Ireland to have electricity. An electric light bulb was installed on the top of the Castle so that local people could see the new wonder. He installed a system of central heating beneath the conservatory. The radiator in the Library was among the original ones used. He also installed a system of plumbing. He panelled the Hall passage in oak and put in doors of oak to the Hall and between the Hall and Drawing Room. In 1892 he died, leaving the place to Helen his eldest daughter.

Helen married Herbert Robertson, later Conservative M.P. for South Hackney, London. He built the Anglican Chapel in 1907 for his wife, and the Brushing Room beneath. The Chapel was under the jurisdiction of the Bishop of Stepney. He also built the greenhouse and acquired the Gate Lodge, the entrance cottages and the Derry House (formerly the barracks of the R.I.C. and later of the Civic Guard). He also constructed the cut granite balcony designed in wrought iron by Manning Robertson. He had the tiles laid on the Tiled Passage and Conservatory floors by some Italian workmen, who it is reported had rows sometimes and fought each other. Herbert also bought out many Headrents. In 1916 he formed the Library, at one time known as the "Red Room". His wife, Helen, only occasionally lived in the castle living mainly in Bristol, where she died in 1932.

In 1926 Helen made over the castle and estate to Manning Durdin Robertson, her eldest son. Towards the end of the 19th Century, according to a report of Manning Robertson, a meteorite fell near the Front Avenue. For two years it glowed and the rooks were very interested in it. No one appears to have moved it. He worked a lot in concrete, building the present green houses with concrete rafters made by himself and Mr. Denis Lacey, also the white Bridge, the kitchen chimney, remodelled the drainage system, built a fountain stem and the front gates and repainted the panelling inside the house and up the main stairs and elsewhere. In 1929 he removed the ivy from and repointed the front of the house. He levelled the lawn immediately in front of the house and moved the tennis court and made it face N.W. and S.E. He removed the battlements and turrets. He bought the sand banks adjoining the Derry near its mouth and laid out the 18 hole golf-course on the banks adjoining the Slaney. In 1927 he, helped by the butler Denis Lacey, built the concrete fishing cabin above the Moss House. He had married, in 1912, Nora, only daughter of Lieut. General Sir L.W. Parsons K.C.B. of the Parsons family of Birr Castle.

## THE GROUNDS

The garden is counted to be the second oldest garden in Ireland. The terraces were laid out by Alexander Durdin in about 1860. Much of the Wilderness was tilled, for root crops. The terraces were dug down about 4 feet and the bank removed by the Rev. Lawrence Durdin-Robertson, who also filled in the path on the South East side of the Castle and the path running from the house to the Centre

Walk. The tennis court on the N. East front of the Castle was removed. In front of the Castle the site of the old Bawn was excavated; a lot of pottery fragments, clay pipes and oyster shells were dug up. The front avenue was continued through the front lawn as far as the Bawn.

The old ruins to the North of the Castle has always been known as the "Abbey". It may have been used by Franciscan monks, or it may have been part of the Augustinian Abbey of Abbeydown, two miles to the East. There are no records (written); it is thought to be over 600 years old. It was kept as a Kennel for harriers, by William Durdin. It has two very old cells, which may have been oratory chapels. They have 3' 6" roofs and date back to the 15th Century. The Yew Walk at the S. East of the Castle, is thought to have been planted by monks. It is a line of 120 English Yew Trees 130 yards long, believed to be over 600 years old. The largest tree is 41' high, and 12'9" wide. An old summer house known as 'the Temple' was in the North East of the terrace and was thatched; the belvedere was built from fragments in 1986 by Lawrence and David Durdin-Robertson. The corners of the Yew Walk, in the East and South were cut down by H. Robertson to give a view from the Castle. The Florence Court Yews on the lawn were originally in the shape of coffee cups, then balls, and then allowed to grow in their natural shape. About 20 fan palms (chamerops) were planted from 1903 onwards by Manning Robertson, who also planted the Pinus Insignis, above the horse pond, and the grove of cypresses.

Mrs. Manning Robertson planted the witch hazel Hammamelis Mollis in front of the Tapestry Room window, in place of the monkey puzzle (Araucaria), the flowering cherry to the left of the Abbey wall, the Mahonia to the right of the Conservatory, the white tree Heather opposite the Tapestry Room window.

Lawrence Durdin-Robertson put in the circular flower bed opposite the Tapestry Room, and then two at the S.W. of the terrace and at the N.E. in place of the old fountain. He also excavated the front terrace, digging down about 4 feet to some foundation walls of the old Bawn, immediately in front of the Castle. The Bawn originally had 11 foot high walls. The wall at the North East of the terrace is thought to be a continuation of the Old Abbey.

# THE TEMPLE OF ISIS

# VIVIENNE O'REGAN

THOSE who are able to journey to the Temple of Isis at Clonegal Castle will have the experience of a lifetime; a rare chance to catch a glimpse of what life may have been like in the mystery temples of Egypt, Greece and Rome. The Temple has been assembled in the spirit and style of the ancient temples, and the most vital thing to remember is that it is not a museum or relic of the ancient goddesses and gods, but a living working temple, alive with music, incense, colour and love.

It celebrates the diversity and the unity of the pantheons and honours worldwide religious traditions.

Within the temple are 26 shrines. Set in a winding pattern throughout the main sanctuary, nave, and chapel of Brigid are found the shrines dedicated to the twelve signs of the Zodiac. There are also five chapels, each one dedicated to the 'philosophical' elements of Earth, Air, Fire, Water and Spirit. Additional shrines are placed in these chapels.

The shrines are not static. Although in the main the central images remain constant, they change as visiting members from all over the world will often present a gift to the Temple. The fact that new things are constantly added or re-arranged means that there is always something new to discover and appreciate about the shrines. My descriptions that follow are in the manner of snapshots taken at a particular time.

The Temple is approached through ornately carved doors that swing open. In an alcove by the entrance stands the tall, white form of an Ibis, a representation of the Egyptian god Thoth, Guardian of the mysteries. Stone steps lead down to a landing. Directly in front upon the wall is a symbol of the Goddess in bright metal which shines as light reflects it, beckoning you down. Beneath it is a plaque depicting Jesus receiving water from the woman at Jacob's well. Underneath are collected various tokens which indicate the diverse nature of the Fellowship as inclusive of all traditions where the Divine Feminine is honoured.

To the left is another pair of swinging doors and a few steps which lead into the main Temple area. Everywhere your eyes turn are images of Goddesses.

Directly ahead is an iron barred gate which leads to the ancient Well of the Castle. To the left of the gate is a huge Tibetan bell which is rung to signify that someone is entering the sacred Temple. During the seasonal ritual celebrations and other formal occasions, it is rung for some time to signify to those gathering that the ceremony is to begin. Smaller bells hang on the right of the gate. Again these are sounded to announce the presence of celebrants and visitors to the Temple.

The interior portion of the Temple measures 79' by 40'. It is built of undressed granite comprising the basement of the original 1625 structure.

The Temple contains a large sanctuary and nave with a row of 9 stone pillars. Two brick pillars stand before the High Altar along with a low brick surround which creates the sanctuary. There is a low raised stone dais before the High Altar on which those of the priesthood stand to make invocation.

## The High Altar of Isis

The High Altar is the central focus of ceremonial activity within the Temple. Its central image is of Isis of Ten Thousand Names. The figure was carved for the Fellowship by David, the Rev. Lawrence Durdin-Robertson's son. Indeed upon the majority of the Temple's shrines are placed David's breathtaking carvings of various goddesses.

The figure is carved from a pale wood and stands around 2ft high. In recent years the figure has been gilded a pale gold. The face of the carving is stunningly alive and upon Her head She bears a pitcher of water in the manner of the Water-bearer of Aquarius emphasising her role as the Goddess of the Aquarian Age.

Isis stands within a golden canopy topped by a Marian crown that once formed part of a church shrine to the Virgin Mary.

A patterned cloth of gold dresses the centre section of the altar hanging down to the floor. Directly underneath the figure of Isis and covering the area just in front of her is a bright red overcloth with golden embroidered pattern. A small candle within a red sanctuary light is placed before her and is always lit during rituals and meditations.

Two sections flank the central altar and upon these are placed a number of sacred objects including the wand of the resident Hierophant and a Marian crown that she wears during ritual observances.

The side altars are dressed with red cloths and in front of each hang golden cloths with a border of red and blue. Upon these side altars stand images of African Goddesses presented to the Temple by Nigerian members. Each stand upon wooden plinths. To the left is an ebony and gold representation of Queen Tahani, legendary ruler of the lost continent of Mu and to the right a wooden statue of Ngame, Creator Goddess of the Nigerian tradition.

To the right of the altar there are windows within the Temple, stained glass motifs in a classic blue and gold pattern. Large vases stand before these two windows filled with flowers and the deep ledges are filled with tokens such as crystals and feathers. The windows are called the Windows of Eternity as mirrors have been placed within their niche so that as you look to the left and right within the niche you can 'see forever'.

### The Chapels of the Elements.

The five main chapels as mentioned above have elemental attributions. The first encountered is the Chapel of Brighid containing the ancient Druidic well with healing properties. It is attributed to Water.The Well is 17' deep.

Within this Chapel are found the shrines of Libra, Scorpio, Sagittarius and Capricorn and the Druidic Well itself, as a separate shrine to the healing properties of the waters. The large window to the South of the Well is decorated with stained glass depicting winged cherubs, the model of a ship of Isis and intricately carved motifs on either side in gold leaf. Also to be found is the eight-pointed star of Ishtar/Isis symbolising the Wheel of the Year. Upon the wall next to the Sagittarius shrine is a clay receptacle for holy water decorated with an ankh.

Moving back into the main section of the Temple the sanctuary is located, containing the shrines for Gemini, Taurus, Aries, Pisces and Aquarius.

## The Zodiacal Shrines:

The energies of the shrines may also be experienced by enactment of the rituals in the Fellowship's Liturgy.

### The Shrine of Aries

This shrine is located in a deep alcove to the rear of the sanctuary area. The Egyptian Goddess Bast, Daughter of Isis, Goddess of Joy, Bounty, Healing and the Dance, is depicted in the form of an upright seated cat carved in wood and stained piebald black and brown. The statue gazes outward towards the High Altar with large black eyes. A necklace of tiger's eye and a golden locket has been placed around the figure's neck. Bast also wears delicate earrings and a green jewel is placed upon her brow. The figure stands on a slightly raised platform surrounded by vases filled with red and pink carnations and other offerings.

Behind the image is a large burnished golden plate, representing the Sun; just above this is a silver mirrored plate representing the Moon. In Egyptian mythology Bast is said to be goddess of both Sun and Moon.

High up in the back of the shrine is a small latticed window which looks out on the Healing Chapel. To the left upon the castle wall is a hanging depicting Amon-Ra the ram-headed god of Egypt. Above the alcove is a plaque depicting the other goddess of this shrine, the Isis of the Palms.

To the shrine of Aries is attributed the FOI ritual of Aries and Durga, the fierce Hindu Goddess. The rite also calls upon the powers of the Grecian Goddess of Wisdom and Justice, Pallas Athena. This is a purification ritual wherein the celebrants face the destructive and aggressive energies within and with the Goddess's help re-direct them towards constructive, life-affirming ends.

## The Shrine of Taurus

Originally this shrine was dedicated to Hathor, the Egyptian Cow Goddess associated with the constellation of Taurus. It is located in the second large alcove opposite the Sanctuary. In 1988 the original shrine underwent a transformation as Olivia was inspired by the visit of an American Priestess-Hierophant who was deeply involved with the Native American and Shamanic traditions. She and Olivia worked together to create in the centre of the shrine a medicine wheel reflecting the rich native traditions of the Americas. There is a Cherokee Iseum in Ohio.

Its central image is of the Goddess Maya, painted by Olivia Robertson following a visionary experience connected with the constellation of Taurus and the pyramids of Egypt and South America. She describes the experience in her introduction to Sophia: "I myself was given a vision related to this part of the sky, the Hyades and Pleiades, and was shown a luminous copper-coloured Goddess with long black hair, seated cross-legged, Her South American Indian face seen in profile. I was given Her name, Maya."

The painting placed on the back wall depicts this Goddess as in the vision, floating in space before a huge golden Sun; above her are the stars of the vision and below her the sphere of the Earth with the continents of South and North America shown.

The floor of the alcove has been covered with stone slabs, placed one on top of the other to create a step effect. White clothes cover the stone and a variety of sacred objects are laid out in the intricate pattern of the medicine wheel. Hand woven and embroidered cloths have been placed over the white cloths and upon them are found a variety of objects, including rattles, smudge sticks, crystals, stones, feathers, beads, a box containing other objects, shells and silver bowls. The candlesticks chosen for this shrine curve out in a 'S' shape.

A figure of the God Quetzalcoatl of South America stands towards the back of the shrine. Upon the left wall is a trellis with silk roses threaded through it and to the right is a buff-coloured hanging decorated with feathers and showing stylised buffalo. To Taurus is attributed the ritual of Taurus and Isis. In this ritual, Isis is invoked as the Bestower of Love and asked that She show the participants the Path of Love for all Creation. The interconnectedness of all life upon the Earth is celebrated.

## The Shrine of Gemini

Dedicated to the Egyptian twin goddess and god, Tefnut and Shu, Goddess of the Dawn and Dew and God of the Air.

The Gemini shrine consists of a church offertory. It is adorned with angelic figures in brass and has places for about 33 candles. Candles are regularly lit by Olivia and Lawrence and their guests with prayers and intentions for healing and other assistance. Here an acknowledgement of new Fellowship members is made by the lighting of a candle symbolising the kindling of the light of the Goddess within their hearts.

The offertory is adorned with a collection of photographs of FOI groups world-wide.

To the Gemini shrine is attributed the Liturgy ritual of Gemini, Artemis and Apollo, Greek twin deities of the Moon and Sun. This ritual again states the universal theme of the divine twins and comprises a quest for Inner Truth and the eventual recognition of the bi-polarity of each soul, whatever physical gender we now incarnate as.

## The Shrine of Cancer

Central to this shrine is a white marble figure of the Goddess Juno. This ancient Italian Goddess became during Roman times the Supreme Goddess and wife of Jupiter, Ruler of the Gods. Like the Greek Goddess Hera, another ancient Goddess whose mythology was later wedded to that of Zeus, King of Olympian gods, with whom She is often associated, Juno is a Goddess of women and the mysteries of womanhood.

The shrine is set back in a rough stone niche. Juno stands on a small stone slab. Before her is a shell filled with tiny treasures including crystals and small shells. Above and behind her is another

Marian crown, a jewelled heart in silver surrounded by a starburst with an array of 11 silver jewelled stars.

Below the shrine hangs an applique cloth representing the spider goddess Arachne. In jewel-like colours it depicts an eight-pointed star with a upward-turning crescent Moon (the Tattvic symbol for Water) with the pale moon spider in its centre. A painting at the very back of the shrine in blue and white depicts the full Moon.

To Cancer is attributed the FOI liturgy ritual of Cancer and Tiamat, the Assyro-Babylonian primordial Sea-Mother Goddess, in which the depths of the seas are contemplated as the origins of life and the Goddess as creatrix of the galaxies and stars.

## The Shrine of Leo

The shrine is dedicated to Venus, Roman Goddess of Love and Beauty and Sekhmet, the Egyptian Lioness Goddess representing the heat of the Sun. The shrine stands flush with the wall of the nave and is comprised of what appears to have been an ebony fireplace. It was carved by Alexander Durdin, the co-founders' great grandfather.

In its upper portion sits the golden image of Bast, the cat Goddess. On either side of Bast is ornamental work of six golden balls atop graceful stems and four fleur-de-lis. The end sections of the fireplace resemble turreted towers.

In the centre of the lower wooden shelf is a carved torso of a voluptuous naked woman representing Venus/Aphrodite, carved by David in Yew. Two pedestals of wood, carved by William Morris, stand alongside the fireplace. Brass lions lie on these facing inward to the shrine.

On the top of the fireplace are the usual two candlesticks with white candles. Between the candles is a Chinese picture, gold on black velvet, depicting a lion-demon and goddess figure. Also to be found is a decorative red candle with a golden image of Sekhmet crowned. Also placed on the top of the shrine is a bell in the shape of a cobra and two red Chinese pots filled with poinsettias.

To the shrine of Leo is attributed the ritual of Leo and Sekhmet. In the ritual the Lion Goddess is invoked and She grants, through the symbolism of the seven Gates of the chakras, her gifts of strength, courage and greatness of heart.

## The Shrine of Virgo

The shrine is found in a small niche in the wall to the right of the Chapel of the Mothers just as you enter the Temple from the stairs. It is dedicated to Isis and Osiris and other small figures of Egyptian gods accompany them. Once again the central image is a wooden carving depicting Isis. She stands quite straight, her right arm raised in a Egyptian ritual salute. Flanking her is a small onyx figure of Bast and a golden figure of the God Khephera. Before her lies the mummified form of her brother and husband, Osiris.

The image of Isis is decorated with gold and strands of wheat lay upon her dais. The floor of the niche is decorated with an intricately patterned cloth in predominantly orange, gold, red and green. A large patterned Ankh hangs down in front of the shrine and cartouches. Upon the walls of the niche are found a number of prints depicting the Goddesses Isis, two by the artist Chesca Potter and another by the sculptor and artist, Ian McDonald.

To the shrine of Virgo is attributed the FOI Ritual of Virgo and Dana, the Irish Mother Goddess. In this ritual the Treasures of the Tuatha De Danann are contemplated as symbolic of the cosmic gifts bestowed by the Gods.

## The Shrine of Libra

This shrine is the first encountered on your left as you pass through the iron gate into the Chapel of Brighid. It is dedicated to the Muses, the nine sister goddesses of Greece who are patrons and inspirers of all the arts and sciences. The central image is a wooden figure of Urania, the Muse of astronomy. She is depicted as a naked woman, her arms upraised in the dance.

The shrine sits within a stone niche and behind it is a William Morris panel with an inlaid gold fleur-de-lis pattern. Soft green material drapes the shrine and frames the walls of the niche. The figure stands upon a wooden dais and beside her is a small gong in the shape of an Ibis, the animal associated with learning in Egypt as the god Tahuti (Thoth). Also upon the shrine is found a long scalloped dish with a rose pattern, and a pompadour with dog-rose scent.

Of course, the most important factor about the Temple is that it is in constant use for meditation and ritual. Both Lawrence and Olivia Durdin-Robertson maintain a daily routine which includes healing, and attunement with members world-wide. Here too, is received the inspiration for the ceremonies and rituals of the Fellowship mediated by Olivia. Clonegal is a special place, and its magic runs deep. The beauty, wisdom and compassion which flow from the Temple of Isis into the world will have repercussions beyond the life-times of its present members.

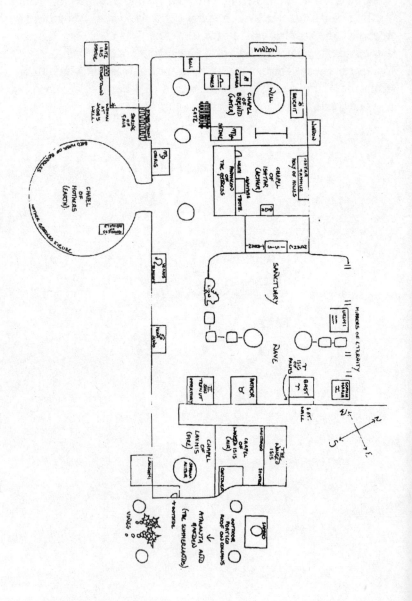